Legalpreneur

THE BUSINESS OWNER'S

GUIDE TO LEGALLY

PROTECTING

YOUR BUSINESS

Andrea Sager

Paperback ISBN: 979-8-9875279-0-0
Hardcover ISBN: 979-8-9875279-1-7
Ebook ISBN: 979-8-9875279-2-4

First paperback edition, 2022
www.thelegalpreneur.com

To my children, Thomas and Allie:
May you always live life according to your heart's deepest desire,
love yourself radically, and fulfill your wildest dreams.

Table of Contents

INTRODUCTION

There I was, a newly minted attorney sitting in the ***office of my dreams***. Since my first year of law school, I have worked towards this moment. This goal drove every late-night, practice test and networking event. It's a coveted opportunity for most law graduates to start their careers at a prestigious Big Law firm. It's the box you're told to fit into from your first day as a law student because it's the golden ticket to the career of your dreams.

But if that were the case, why was I sitting in a thousand-dollar chair overlooking the Cincinnati Reds baseball stadium, daydreaming about what it would feel like to walk out of this office, get into my car and never look back? It wasn't the notoriously long hours. I worked full-time throughout law school while mothering my infant son. I was used to 14-hour days. It was something else. Regardless of how hard I tried, how hard I worked, or how well I fit in with the other associates, the person I had learned to suppress was screaming to be released. This wasn't where I was supposed to be, and my body knew it before my mind would accept it.

I lasted eight months—way longer than I thought I would. Then fate happened.

I got fired.

It was like the universe heard everything I had been quietly manifesting and decided to give me a little nudge in the direction I needed most. Because sometimes, what holds us back is our need to be in control. We desire comfort, stability and the safety that comes with knowing where our next paycheck comes from. But like my mentor Chris Harder always says, good is the enemy of great. And being comfortable was keeping me away from tapping into my greatness.

Truthfully, I had been flirting with the idea of quitting long before that fateful day. Here's how it happened. That Monday, my now ex-husband (a stay-at-home dad at the time) and I decided to put our house on the market. He knew I was unhappy, and that I had dreams beyond the walls of what a typical first-year law associate was told to aspire to. Selling our home was phase one of my safely planned and carefully measured exit strategy. There was no room for risks and jumping in with both feet. Or so I thought. That Wednesday, I texted my ex-husband in the middle of the work day and told him I needed out. I wasn't up to waiting for the house to sell or for another associate position to come my way. I was miserable, and I couldn't afford it anymore. I needed to change our plans. We had enough saved to tie us over for a little while. He asked me to wait, until we had a contract pending on our home. As a mother of a 1-year-old, and the sole provider, I couldn't afford to only think about my happiness. Although I agreed to not quit until we had a contract on our home, the universe conspired to show me that it was time for me to pursue something else.

Now it was Friday morning. I knew the moment my mentor and the firm's then-managing partner walked into my office. What I didn't know was how things would work in my favor. Very few, if any, first-year associates celebrate being let go. I was one of the very few. I was offered two choices – I could go on a three-month probation or take a severance package. I tried not to let the glimmer in my eye show when I heard the number. Here I was, trying to convince myself I needed to stay in a job I hated to take care of my family. But the universe showed me that was far from the truth.

I don't remember how I left the office. In my head, I was over the moon. I had let fear and external expectations dictate my steps for so long. As much as I spent months romanticizing what it would feel like to quit and pursue the dreams calling to me, I was too afraid to pull the trigger. It wasn't because I was unsure of myself. I knew firsthand what I was capable of. I grew a business from my Poshmark storefront to a small e-commerce store to a profitable brick and mortar while dealing with the pressures of law school. I knew my strengths and played them well.

But like many of us, I was terrified to go against the grain. It wasn't thoughts of failure that paralyzed me. It was the fear of what others would think. Big Law firms only hire the top students. From the first day of law school, you're taught that the smart students go into Big Law, and everyone else aspires to get there one day. This is what I was supposed to aspire to. I was scared and afraid to do what made me happy, because I was worried about what people would think. You would expect that getting fired would have triggered those insecurities. Instead, it gave me the freedom to show up as myself and practice the law in ways that excited me.

Guess what happened next?

Our house was sold with an all-cash offer. Then, I launched my own law firm. Almost overnight, the life I wanted was becoming more than a mid-day dream. It became what I woke up to, day in and day out. You see, the problem was never the law. I love being a lawyer. I love working with my clients to come up with creative solutions to legal issues, and I especially love helping them grow their businesses. It's the stuff that gets me up in the morning – truly. But I was never meant to be a traditional attorney because I'm not a traditional person. And let's be honest, neither are you. As a small business owner, you decided to leap without knowing where you would land. You went against the grain not because you wanted to but because you had to. Thinking of the alternative of not showing up in this world exactly as you are, would have eaten away at you.

Throughout these pages, I'll walk you through everything you need to know about creating a legally legit business that protects you, your assets, and the life you were meant to live.

This is more than just another business book. It's a guide on how to create and sustain your legacy. Because that's what all of this is, right? What we do every day is the mark that we will eventually leave on this world. That thought was nagging at me while working at my old firm. Is this really it for me? Is this what I was called to do? We can distract ourselves from listening to our inner voice, but that feeling never goes away. Eventually, it bubbles to the surface and tears down all the limiting beliefs you once held. If you're reading this book, congratulations – it means you decided to listen to the voice that was telling you there is so much more to *you*.

Here's a secret: there's no one way to do business. Sure, there are blueprints and general structures you can follow. But what makes a business successful is the heart and soul that runs it. I'm talking about *you*. There's a reason I was able to scale from selling on Poshmark to owning a storefront in less than two years. It wasn't the money I was pouring into my business, a large marketing firm, or overzealous sales funnels. It was me. Yes, I followed the general structures of how to run a business. No amount of personality can circumvent the importance of a business plan or the proper legal entity. But that's just the skeleton. I ran my businesses in ways that felt authentic to me. That's how I attracted my customers, gained referrals and made my mark on social media. It's also how I started a million dollar law firm within two years of graduating from law school.

After getting fired, I could have let myself believe I wasn't cut out to be a lawyer. Imposter syndrome usually does a pretty good job of convincing us that our failures are indicative of our strengths. I chose to fall forward though. Isn't that what being a good business owner is all about? We position ourselves as individuals choosing to see failures as falling forward, until you get to the door that opens for you. I was meant to be a lawyer. I just wasn't meant to be that kind of lawyer, and that's perfectly okay. Going to law school, passing the bar and being admitted is the skeleton of becoming an attorney. However, everything else? Every external expectation of the firm you're supposed to work at or what clerkship you're supposed to take is background noise. The beliefs that you have on how to run a successful business? I'm here to show you that a lot of it is probably background noise as well.

I created my signature legal framework Legalpreneur Inc. because many of us were socialized into internalizing limiting beliefs that are counter to who we are as people. And the world really needs more of us who are unafraid to show up as ourselves. Throughout this book, I'll walk you through the steps you need to take as a business owner. Because before you can fill in the skeleton, you first need to understand it.

And let me tell you why I'm the best person to help you do that.

My name is Andrea Sager - founder of Andrea Sager Law, Legalpreneur, and the Dream Bigger conference. I've founded, scaled and sold multiple six and seven-figure businesses in various industries, including fashion and technology. I love motivational speeches, and big audacious goals, and I freaking love playing poker. In fact, I love it so much that one time I decided to buy a poker club because I spent so much time there. It ended up being a fantastic investment that I sold for a return 10x the purchase price in less than a year.

I'm a mother of two beautiful children, and they used to be my why – the driving force behind each of my overly ambitious goals. But then I realized that I can only fully step into my power when I am the reason. Not my children, not my parents and definitely not society. Me, Andrea. Both the young girl I was and the woman I became. It took me a long time to get here. To act consistently from a place of raw authenticity, a story that we will touch on more in the book. But I stated all of that to say:

How many times do we act in hopes of inspiring others to dream bigger, reach further, and live their fullest potential? It's a beautiful thought, but if we are constantly acting for the sake of others, when can we show up for ourselves? When do we fulfill our purpose? Make no mistake, my children are still the heartbeat of my actions, but they are not the reason. I am. The most powerful legacy you can leave behind is an authentic life. And that's why I do this for my children, my community and the women that come after me.

There is no one way to be a business owner. No matter what you see on your social media feed or on the cover of magazines.

If you sell products or services, congratulations, you own a business. No more playing small and treating it like a hobby – there's so much more to you than that. And I'm here to help you each step of the way.

Here's to building something memorable together.

How To Use This Book

Think of these pages as a manual to come back to again and again. With personal stories, lessons learned from clients, and a step-by-step breakdown of running a business, I want you to use this book to succeed in life, love, business, and everything in between. Take notes. Write in the margins. Use it in your business masterminds or book clubs. No matter where you are in your entrepreneurial journey, the topics covered in *The Legalpreneur* book will help you get from where you are to where you want to be.

There are resources throughout, including client case studies, testimonials, and contract templates to support you in elevating your business. But, as thorough as this book is, it's also just the beginning. Legal issues are complex, intricate and fact specific. In other words, everything you need to know cannot be covered on these pages. The good news is that I have a team of lawyers ready to help you if you need additional support. Just say when.

For now, start here. I can't wait to see you grow.

Chapter 1:
The Beginning

"Make something people want" includes making a company that people want to work for." — *Sahil Lavingia*

There's something to be said about new beginnings. It's infatuating how even the thought of a new endeavor can completely transform the energy in your day. Perhaps it's the symbolism that we love. The proverbial pull of a fresh start, a clean slate and the suggested promise of an abundance of opportunities. Who wouldn't love a do-over? If only it were that easy.

Here's the thing. There's a shelf-life for everything. Your ideas and the fervent excitement that drives most of us when we're inspired to take action and create are limited. It will fade. That's inevitable because there's no longevity in a spark. Unless, of course, you innovate from a place of inspiration. This book will help you do that if you allow it to.

I wrote this book for you - for every business owner who has ever doubted themselves. For every parent who's ever considered starting a business so they could spend more time with their children. For the dreamers, the doers and the believers. For the unconventional person who refused to take no for an answer. This book is about to become your new best friend.

Between these pages, you'll find a step-by-step guide that will support you in prospering as an entrepreneur. You'll also find stories that I hope will inspire you when you are feeling stuck, confused or overwhelmed.

Let's get started by looking at your business roots.

The Foundation

Maybe I'm a little biased, but I think this is the most critical chapter and not just because it will teach you how to set up your business structure. The chapter is important because it pairs business structure with mindset, which creates the foundations of your business.

Typically, you are taught that there are seven things to consider when starting a business. They are:

1. Business Plan
2. Business Structure
3. Insurance and Liability
4. Understanding Your Market
5. Who to Hire
6. Utilizing Contracts
7. Accounting

But in this book, there's an eighth – your mindset.

Get Your Head Right, Get Your Bread Right (Or Something Like That)

I tell all my clients to start here because listen, your mind is the most powerful tool you have. Our thoughts control our actions, whether we think them consciously or not. That means what you think about yourself as an individual and as a business owner will ultimately impact the outcome of your company. For example, if you frequently find yourself stuck in patterns of negative self-talk, it's likely that these thoughts will manifest into self-sabotaging behavior, including perfectionist tendencies and over-analysis paralysis. None of this does you any good. If anything, it will deter you from continuing your business when things get a bit rocky. Why go all in on something if you are convinced it will fail? (Hint: the answer is you won't.)

It happens slowly, and I've seen it enough times to know when my clients are veering into dangerous territory. It goes a little something like this:

- Client gets excited about a new project/product/business model.
- Dives in head first and launches.
- Initial excitement wears off, and the *oh shit* moment sets in. Client starts to second-guess themselves. Instead of excitement, the client is filled with dread and worry.

- The first few weeks or months of business were great, but now the client is worried they can't replicate that success. They are paralyzed by this thought.
- They begin to brainstorm new ideas for future launches and social content. But instead of taking action, they stall.
- Their inner critic is telling them this isn't a good idea. The idea is too basic and there is no point in launching a new project.
- Cracks show. Eventually, the client ignores emails, misses deadlines, and starts dropping the ball on routine tasks.
- Client starts making excuses and becomes hypercritical of the work product. They stop putting work out because nothing feels "good enough."
- Anxiety sets in. Client continues to ignore business needs, all while continuously producing new work.
- Business fails.

Your insecurities will talk you out of a million-dollar idea if you allow it. The trick is to tackle these limiting beliefs before they paralyze you.

I'm speaking from experience here because this is not an unfamiliar cycle. Early in my career, I learned that being done was better than perfect. Every time I wanted to obsess over a small detail or fixate on an aspect of my business that didn't seem right, my hesitation reflected my inner world. It's not that my product wasn't ready, it's that I wasn't ready. I wasn't prepared to face the possibility of failure, stagnation or needing to go back to the drawing board.

Because let's face it, there's something terrifying about putting yourself out there and learning that what you're sharing is "not good enough" or that people don't like it. As much as we know we shouldn't, we tend to see any shortcomings as a reflection of who we are and what we are worth rather than as an indicator of where we can improve. And if you're someone who grew up in a hyper-critical environment, multiply that fear of failure ten times over. We've all been kept up at night with "what if" scenarios, whether it's before a massive change in our life, the first day at a new job, or the night before a big launch. But what sense does it make to be afraid of the unknown? Essentially, you're setting yourself up for failure before you know what's out there. So don't quit before you've gotten started.

Begin by exploring what your inner voice sounds like and whom you've modeled it after. In most cases, how we speak to ourselves reflects how our primary caregiver engaged with us. How were you cared for as a child? How were you spoken to, and how do you speak to yourself now?

While these questions may not seem related to running a business, they absolutely are. How we were treated as children, reflects in how we speak to ourselves as adults. The next time you feel overwhelmed, afraid or indecisive before making a business decision, check in with yourself. What is your inner dialogue saying, and whose voice is that? If you find yourself becoming hypercritical, negative, or outright mean to yourself, that's an indicator that you have some work to do. Parse through your inner thoughts the next time your subconscious mind runs wild, and stay engaged. Question what you are telling yourself, and ask if what your inner voice is saying is true. Remind yourself that the negative beliefs you have aren't yours, and that you are destined to succeed if you allow yourself to believe that.

Here Are Some Journal Prompts That Might Help:

1. When I feel overwhelmed, I…
2. What am I most afraid of?
3. I am proud of myself when…
4. My inner dialogue is…
5. Success makes me feel…

How Self-Sabotage Can Show Up

This one is major. Something that I think about often is this quote by Marianne Williamson in her award-winning book, *A Return to Love: Reflections on the Principles of A Course in Miracles.*

"Our deepest fear is not that we are inadequate. Our deepest fear is that we are powerful beyond measure. It is our light, not our darkness that most frightens us. We ask ourselves, 'Who am I to be brilliant, gorgeous, talented, fabulous?' Actually, who are you not to be? You are a child of God. Your playing small does

not serve the world. There is nothing enlightened about shrinking so that other people won't feel insecure around you. We are all meant to shine, as children do. We were born to manifest the glory of God that is within us. It's not just in some of us; it's in everyone. And as we let our own light shine, we unconsciously give other people permission to do the same. As we are liberated from our own fear, our presence automatically liberates others."

Somewhere in our lives, we were taught that playing small and dimming our light is safer. But who does that serve? Sure, it may keep the people around us more comfortable, but in keeping them comfortable, you're also keeping them stuck. Do you remember a time when you were made to feel bad for being really good at something or really passionate? For some of us, it happened in grade school.

Think about it – when was it ever cool to be really good at something? If you were academically gifted, you were bullied. If you were kind and empathic to the teacher, you were a teacher's pet. If you were passionately and enthusiastically involved in class discussions in law school, you were a gunner. And believe me, no one wanted to be a gunner. So, why did we allow ourselves to think that it was cool not to care and to half-ass our way through life?

If you're reading this, I need you to promise me, and more importantly, yourself this one thing – you're going to do this for real. You will go all in on your business, and take consistent actions to build the company you've always been capable of.

Ready?

We'll talk about a couple more things... and then we will dive into the business side of things. But these are practices I want you to keep coming back to.

Wellness Practices For Entrepreneurs

There are countless blog posts, podcasts and books dedicated to the importance of morning routines for creatives and CEOs. But really, they are essential for everyone. Think of your morning routine as the little things you need to do each day to feel grounded and present in your body. When I was a kid, I was always a little confused when I heard people say they woke up on the wrong side of the bed. Because what does that even mean, right? Did you wake up sideways or with your feet pointing towards the headboard (like my son does), and how did you get there?

Linguistics aside... I eventually learned that what you do before falling asleep and upon waking up has the ability to determine how you operate. Meaning you have the power to decide your day before it even begins. This does not mean you need to force yourself to be a morning person or adopt a daily routine you found on Instagram. Simply put, you need to find what works for you. And stick to these daily habits, even when it gets hard. Actually, scratch that, especially when it gets hard. I always thought it was strange how our daily practices are the first things we toss to the side when we are stressed. We skip meals, opt for fast food when we do eat and forgo the gym, pilates, yoga or whatever it is that best helps keep us grounded. But why is that? If these were practices we developed to clear and ease our minds, isn't a stressful period when we need these tools the most?

We often develop routines for our ideal life. The problem is that as an entrepreneur, your schedule may not accommodate for ideal. I always tell my clients that the most important routine is the one that they stick to. Commit to something that makes sense to you and works with your schedule. Do not aim for perfection here. Do not expect yourself to wake up at 5 AM if you are not a morning person, run 6 miles if you hate running, journal, meditate, shower, and make breakfast before the kids wake up. Start small and slow, with intention.

- Ask yourself, how do I want to feel before bed at night?
- Then ask, how do I want to feel before I start my day every morning?

How you answer these questions will determine the type of routine you curate for yourself. I know that I have the most restful sleep if I quiet my mind before going to bed. I also have the most productive days when I feel grounded and connected to myself. As a single mom with two children and as a CEO, it's also necessary for me to be realistic about my time. It's called a daily practice for a reason. If your routines are too elaborate for everyday use, you need to consider your strategy.

Again, this is where perfectionists' fantasies come into play. It's not about checking all the boxes and doing everything you see your favorite content creator posting. It's about finding a manageable system that works for you.

Tips For Daily Routines

- Do something for your mind, body and soul. This could include a morning meditation (mind), yoga class (body) and daily journaling practice (soul).
- Give yourself a time limit. Most practices don't stick because we try to build habits and practices based on an ideal life, instead of reality. The truth is, you don't have 3 hours to do an extensive morning routine. Most people with full-time jobs and responsibilities don't. Having a routine that works for you isn't meant to be aesthetically pleasing or transformed into digital content - it's supposed to be helpful. Remember, you are choosing what works for you, not what you saw your favorite content creator do on Instagram.
- Once you decide on a time limit, pick a few things you can commit to every day. My team knows that I go for a walk every morning after dropping off the kids at school and listen to my favorite podcast. Even though my phone is with me, I keep it on do not disturb so that I can have uninterrupted time with myself. It's almost like a solo staff meeting. When I'm done playing poker in the evenings, I incorporate a breathwork practice that helps

me release any stress or tension in my body. I accompany that with a journaling practice. If my morning fills me up with inspiration, my evening is designed to release everything that I'm ready to let go of.

- Change your routine depending on how your body is feeling. I've learned over the years how important it is to do check-ins with myself before starting my practice. If movement is an important part of my mornings or evening, but I'm not feeling up for a walk, I'll modify and give my body a practice that's more aligned with what it's feeling.

Remember that the most important thing in any daily routine is the feeling it leaves you with. So figure out what you need to be productive, energized and focused, and commit to it until it's time to try something else.

It Was All A Dream... Until It Wasn't

I've always been a huge planner. That feeling you get when you buy a new day planner from Target with your favorite pen? Unmatched. It's the perfect blend of organization and inspiration. Almost like the feeling you get when you set a New Year's resolution. In both instances, there's a huge surge of excitement around a specific major goal. But the problem with New Year's resolutions, and even day planners, is the lack of dopamine. Hear me out. Big goals are great. But have you ever wondered why they sometimes seem so challenging to get to? It's because your mind needs a reward system to stay motivated. Aiming to run a marathon at the end of the year is fantastic (and props to you, I've run a half-marathon once), but how will you get there?

Creating mini-goals will help keep you motivated and support you in reaching your bigger goal. For instance, I have a big fitness goal for the end of the year, and I hold myself accountable to it by using a bullet journal. I love seeing workout streaks and creating mini-challenges for myself. This helps me stay on track by breaking my bigger goal into bite-size pieces. It's no longer about running a marathon for me. Now, it's about getting in 5 workouts a week or closing my fitness rings every day. It's fun to compete with yourself. Give it a try.

This works well in business too. Break down your yearly goals into quarters, months, weeks and daily-to-do lists. Let's say you're trying to make $1,000,000 a year. That means you need to make $250,000 per quarter or roughly $83,000 per month. Still a big scary number, but much more manageable than thinking of a 7-figure goal.

What does an $83,000 month look like in your business? Your first few steps might include increasing your rates, decreasing your overhead costs, and outsourcing so you can expand your workload. Next, examine the space between where you are, and where you want to be. What marketing strategies will offer the best ROI? Then, write out your framework. If you need to make a certain amount of money before you can start outsourcing your marketing, that should be a priority goal. Of course, this is all general advice, but take this thought process and apply it to your own business goals.

Goal Setting Summary:

- Write out your one-year business goals.
- Break those goals into smaller bite-sized goals, such as quarterly, monthly and weekly.
- Make your daily to-do lists to support your weekly goals, which in turn support your monthly goals.
- Use active language that's measurable. For example, instead of saying you'll grow your social media, say, "We will have 10,000 Instagram followers by the end of this year." You can break this goal into smaller targets, such as gaining 2,000 followers per month, and then create daily to-do lists supporting this vision.
  - E.g. Monday: shoot content and engage with 100 accounts. Tuesday: research hashtags and post reel. Wednesday: post a writing sample and respond to DMs. (Of course, this is a straightforward to-do list for social media, but you get the idea.)

The Beliefs That Limit Us

If you read any of the above and thought, "Cool idea, but this won't work for me," I want you to ask yourself why. We've all been there; in a place where we seem to think that what works for others, won't work for us. But what if I told you that the problem is your mindset? If you believe things won't work for you, they won't because you carry that energy. So I need you to do me a favor.

I need you to park every negative belief and limiting mindset you have about yourself and go all in here. This book will work for you. Your goals can become your reality. But I need you to believe in yourself here, okay? Because I believe in you. Really, I do. I dedicated my career to small business owners because I believe in your business that much. But I can't help you if you don't believe in yourself too. So we're going to make some magic happen by letting go of the things that hold us back. Trust me, trust yourself, and go all in here.

Let's get started.

Structuring Your Baby

Before diving into the legal protections, there's one thing I need to make sure you understand. You don't have to do any of this. I can't tell you how often someone has asked me, "Is it illegal if I do this or if I do it this way?" Well, 95% of the time it's not illegal, and the feds aren't going to come knocking at your door. Most of what I'm teaching here is how to protect what you're doing. Once you become a business owner, whether you realize you're a business owner or not, your risk dramatically increases. Think of what we're doing here as building a wall of protection around your business.

Each piece of protection is a new layer of bricks. The goal is to have so much protection that no one can get through the wall and harm your business.

First things first, for your business to thrive, you need to treat it like a business. There's no value in playing small. Your online boutique, course, podcast, etc., isn't a *"little hobby."* It's a legal entity that's obligated to file taxes – or at least, it should be. That's what we're here to talk about. The most harmful thing you can do for your business, no matter the size, is to not treat it like one.

With the rise of online retailers and service providers, starting a business has never been more convenient. Aspiring business owners are no longer weighed down by the burdensome responsibility of leasing a storefront, carrying thousands of dollars of merchandise in stock, or employing a rotating staff. There is power in accessibility. There are also consequences. Because of the relative simplicity of setting up an online business, the lines between hobby and business are blurring. The romanticized notion of turning your side hustle into your main hustle has created the assumption that the natural course of action is to grow your hobby into a business.

But why not just start your business as a business? Hear me out.

Case Study: The Power Of Having A Legal Entity

Say you're a software engineer working a traditional 9-5. On the side, you design apps that streamline the pattern grading process for creatives using artificial intelligence. Lately, your apps have become popular in the right circles, and the number of downloads is growing exponentially. This is good news! You planned to eventually leave your 9-5 and launch a tech startup that specialized in merging the worlds of fashion and technology. But because you aren't bringing in much of an income just yet, you haven't thought of a business plan. You also think it's too soon to form a legal entity because what's the point? There isn't a profit for you to be taxed on.

But then the unexpected happens. Investors come knocking. They want to know more about your product because they see the great potential and are considering investing. There's just one problem. You're not a company. You're not even an LLC or a general partnership. But that's okay, right? You'll fix the problem, register your business and be on your way to success with investors backing your every step. Unfortunately, that likely won't be the case. There are dangers that come with playing small, and sometimes the consequence is lost opportunity. And let's be honest, the best way to get ready is to stay ready.

I want to scream when I hear talented creatives or budding entrepreneurs talk down their business and their ambitions.

In life and business, there will be lots of things that try to tear you down. All I ask is that you don't do it yourself. With this example, the entrepreneur only lost the opportunity. But it could have been a lot worse. We'll get to that in the next chapter. But for now, please know you are limiting yourself in more ways than one if you decide to forgo legally structuring your business.

If It Looks Like a Business And Acts Like A Business, Then It's A Business

It is absolutely possible to turn a hobby into a successful business. Between you and I, part of why I struggled with going to work at my previous firm was because my heart wasn't set on servicing major corporations. I care about helping small businesses grow into big businesses. I care about *this* - what we're doing here with this book matters to me. But what happens when you are low on passion, or the drive to deliver isn't there? You've probably seen this play out in your life before. Think of a time when a passion project or an unexpected hobby consumed you for a period. When did it stop? Chances are, once life got busy, your attention span began to wander. And slowly, all at once, the past-time that consumed you a few short weeks prior had been forgotten. You may reach for that top shelf every once in a while and pick up that abandoned past-time back up. But inconsistency is the enemy of progress. Comparably, approaching your business in a similar way would be to your detriment. That's why you need to plan to mitigate inconsistencies, creative lows, and the days when it feels impossible to get to where you're going.

How do you do that? With structure. Hard deadlines are your friends here, as is accountability. One way is to file a legal entity. Make things official and commit to consistently showing up. In addition to helping you elevate how you show up in your business, operating your business under a legal entity protects you financially. It can also save you money come tax season (more on that in chapter two).

If you're self-funding your businesses, I can understand the hesitation in spending limited resources on a costly registration without immediate benefit. But that's just it. It doesn't have to be costly; the longer you wait, the more expensive it will become. Your business is an investment every step of the way. You will receive ten-fold the amount you put into it. You just need to decide whether or not to go all in.

If you're not sure if you have a business, ask yourself these questions:

- Has someone paid you money for doing something for them?
- Has someone paid you money in exchange for items?
- Are you building a structure to accept money for these situations?

If you answered yes to any of the questions above, you probably have a business.

I once had someone making money for a consulting gig, and she kept telling me she wanted to create a business around what she was doing. I had the pleasure of telling her, "Congrats! You already have a business." I know she's not alone in not realizing she already has a business, and I don't want you to make the same mistake.

Decide How To Structure Your Business

The legal structure you choose depends entirely on your business's needs. The good news is that the entity you form now is not binding.

Listed below are the most common options you can choose from:

Sole Proprietorship

This is for the uneducated business owner. Well, maybe. The advantages of a sole proprietorship is its simplicity, and it's probably what you are if you haven't filed any entity documents with your state. If you think you just have a hobby that makes money, you're probably a sole proprietor. It's relatively easy to set up, with minimal overhead costs. But for many businesses, the drawbacks outweigh the potential benefits.

There's no separation between you and your business if you are a sole proprietor. That means your assets are vulnerable to any debts, financial liability or potential litigation you face through your business. As a sole proprietor, you and your business are one and the same. There's no degree of separation, and that's not a good thing. Unfortunately, this is one of the riskier options when it comes to choosing the right entity for your business.

I generally caution against continuing your business as a sole proprietor. I do so because of the unlimited liability and what that could mean for your personal life, even if you later become a different entity. While it's easy to brush off potential legal concerns, especially if you are an online service-based business, remember that our world is changing. Litigation for businesses isn't just slip-and-fall cases. It could also result from posting a Pinterest photo on your Instagram account without permission, even if you give the creator credit.

Pros: Easy to set up, minimal paperwork and affordable (upfront)
Cons: Unlimited personal liability, difficult to raise capital, can cost you 100x more down the road.

Recommended for: Truthfully, no one. The personal risk is too high!

Limited Liability Company (LLC)

LLCs are ordinarily standard for entrepreneurs in both product and service-based professions. Think of this entity as a hybrid. Your assets are protected from potential liability or debt recovery. However, you can also pass any additional business profits and losses onto your income tax return. This is typically the best option for an entity regarding small businesses. Even if you're the sole owner of the business, you want to ensure you have that degree of separation to assure you are not personally liable for your company debts. It may not seem like a big deal to keep the break between you and your business, but you ultimately don't know what will happen. And this little bit of protection can literally save your house, car and other personal assets.

While there is some overlap, the process of forming an LLC varies depending on your state of residence. Here's a brief and general overview of how to file for an LLC.

- **Step One**: Decide where you want to form your LLC. Typically, this should be the primary state where you decide to do business in. I know we've all heard of filing in Delaware or another state with tax benefits. But the benefits typically don't apply if it's a small business. Additionally, if you file in a state other than the one you live in, you will be doing double duty with paperwork, fees, etc.

- **Step Two:** Select your business name and make sure it's available on the Secretary of State's records. You want to make sure another qualified entity is not using it. Do not mistake this with a trademark search, which is much more in-depth.

- **Step Three:** Choose a registered agent. When forming an LLC, you are required to have a registered agent in the state of formation or qualification. So, what's a registered agent? Think of them as the person you would want to receive legal documents on behalf of your LLC. This can be you or a third-party (like Legalpreneur).

- **Step Four:** Prepare an LLC operating agreement. The aforementioned is an agreement between all the members of the LLC and essentially governs how the business will handle disputes between the owners, profits, interest transfers, and all other business-related issues. Even as the sole owner, I highly suggest having one for your business.

Pros: No personal liability. Your personal assets cannot be pursued, even in the case of bankruptcy and pass-through tax benefit.

Cons: Forming an LLC can be more costly than forming a general partnership or a sole proprietorship. It can be difficult to transfer ownership of an LLC with multiple members, or to add additional members.

Recommended For: This is the legal entity that I recommend to most of my clients, who range from photographers to designers, accountants, and everything in between.

Partnership

Unlike LLCs or a corporation, a partnership does not require any official filing, nor does it have legal status. It's simply an agreement, written or unwritten, between two or more parties to do business together, and share in profits and losses.

Pros: It's easy to form and has no expensive paperwork.

Cons: You share liability with all of the other partners and can be responsible for the actions of another partner.

Recommended For: Anyone doing business with another person or business and not as adept at filing an LLC.

Corporation

A corporation is a distinct legal entity owned by its shareholders. It can have its own assets and has legal rights and liabilities. In a corporation, shareholders are protected from personal liability for actions taken on behalf of the corporation. However, the CEO can still be held liable for certain actions of the company

For the most part, I don't suggest a corporation to small business owners. There are more fees, maintenance, and taxes involved, and you get the same liability protection as an LLC. A corporation is typically best for companies planning to have investors or raise money. If you plan on raising venture capital or private equity funding, you will 100% need a corporation.

Here's how to form a corporation.

- **Step One**: Appoint a registered agent and file articles of incorporation. The agent must be a resident of the state that you are filing.

- **Step Two**: Draft corporate bylaws and appoint directors. Think of your bylaws as your internal guiding document. It defines the rights and responsibilities of the shareholders and directors and outlines the corporate procedure.

- **Step Three**: Issue stock to shareholders who have contributed cash, services or other resources to the company.

Pros: No personal liability for shareholders or directors, access to capital, and the business operates in continuity.

Cons: Costly to form, subject to double taxation and heavy regulation.

Recommended For: Larger businesses looking to attract investors and issue stocks.

There's a lot to think about when choosing a legal entity. So here are a few things to think about when deciding which structure works best for you and your business:

1. Will I be a solopreneur?
2. What is the nature of my business?
3. How much capital do I need to get started?
4. Am I interested in working with investors?
5. What are my financial goals over the next five years?
6. What is my projected income for this year?

Remember, your legal entity is allowed to change as your business grows. For now, make the decision that best protects you, your business, and the goal you're working towards.

An LLC is typically the best option for small business owners like you. If you need help filing your LLC, go to thelegalpreneur.com.

Chapter 2:
Business Structure, Taxes, and Insurance

"Dear IRS, I am writing to you to cancel my subscription. Please remove my name from your mailing list." — Snoopy

Tax season is a ritual I have always found comfort in, maybe because it's a constant. It's a marker of time, seasons and change. We welcome the warmer weather each year with spring cleaning and filing our taxes. It's the most wonderful time of the year – sort of. Truthfully, I went to law school intending to become a tax attorney. I'm a numbers girl, very analytical, and there are few things I love as much as a numerical puzzle. Imagine my surprise when I realized not everyone feels the same way. Anxiety around taxes? Who knew? (Seriously, I had no idea.) Then, during my first tax season as a solo practitioner, I realized that many people dread filing their taxes because they don't realize it's just a game.

Before you roll your eyes and glaze over this chapter, give me a chance. By the end of this chapter, I promise that, you too, will begin to get excited about tax season.

A Real-Life Video Game

I like to think of filing taxes as a nationwide, year-long episode of extreme couponing. The category? Life. As a business owner, when you start paying attention to what you can claim as a tax expense, you realize how every aspect of your day-to-day life could be considered a business expense. Sounds made up, right? How can dinner with your partner be a tax right off? Simple – it starts with your business structure. In the previous chapter, we discussed the importance of setting up your business as a legal entity. Now, I'm going to show you why setting up a business structure is so important.

Understanding Your Business Needs

Here's the thing – everything depends on your business structure, from how you run it, when you file your taxes, and what you can write off. I never recommend taking shortcuts or cutting corners, but I definitely advise against it when deciding which business structure is best for your company. My advice? Take the time to determine what business structure makes the most sense for you because making the wrong decision could cost you during tax season. The good news is that it's possible to change your business structure after filing. The bad news is it's an expensive mistake to make.

There are numerous factors to consider when deciding how to structure your business. But ultimately, it comes down to revenue and liability. For tax purposes, revenue is the driving force. However, the two are inseparable in deciding how to file, and the two should be considered simultaneously.

What Is Liability?

Liability is a company's financial debts or obligations that arise during the course of business. In some instances, it can include the owner's personal liability, meaning their assets outside the business. This is one of the many reasons it's so critical to understand the risks and needs of your business – you could be putting your home, car, and life savings on the line. So, how do you prevent that? By operating your business under the appropriate business structure.

Liability is one of the reasons I often push back against new clients who want to be a sole proprietor or file a Doing Business As (DBA). If you have little to no assets or believe your business is low-risk for a lawsuit, it may be an attractive choice – but I still highly caution against it. Just because you do not have assets at the time of the incident does not mean your future possessions are safe. In many instances, the injured party can file a claim against you up to three years or more after the incident. That means anything you've acquired in that time is at risk.

Corporations offer the most protection against personal liability. However, it's costly and not always worth it. This is why I recommend small businesses that operate primarily in the U.S. operate under a limited liability company. An LLC is a business entity created by state statutes that permit the pass-through federal tax treatment of a sole proprietorship if there is only one owner. If there is more than one owner, the tax treatment is the same as a partnership, which is usually not ideal, but you still have options, which we will discuss later in this chapter. Additionally, the LLC provides the owners with the limited liability protections of a corporation. Meaning you get the best of the best – protection of your personal assets, the flexibility of your tax structure, and fewer fees and maintenance as a corporation.

You Thought We Were Finished?

There's a lot more to say about business structures. And while I could go on and on explaining the differences between them, it may be more efficient if we review the most frequently asked questions for each entity.

LLCs And Taxes: Here's Everything You Need To Know

"I heard I shouldn't file an LLC until I'm making $100,000 in my business."

I've talked to several clients who've said they've had accountants tell them that they do not need to worry about filing an LLC until they make more money. Please, believe me when I say that is the wrong answer. In my opinion, you need to become an LLC as soon as possible because its sole purpose is to limit your liability. The LLC isn't just to protect your future earnings as a business owner. It's to safeguard what you personally own now. That includes your house, car, liquid assets and everything else you own. If you do not file an LLC, and your business is sued, it doesn't matter whether or not your business is making money because they are going to come after you personally. However, if you have an LLC, your business is sued, and you're not bringing in any money, the party suing you is straight out of luck. They cannot come for your personal assets as an LLC, unless something is allowing them to "pierce the corporate veil." Piercing the corporate veil is a phrase used in business when a business owner has not maintained the requirements of staying in compliance with the business entity. If this happens, you lose the veil of protection that an LLC or a corporation provides, and the other party can come after your personal assets. One of the most common ways this happens is when funds are being commingled. Meaning you mixed your personal and professional money.

Accountants tell people to wait until they're making a certain dollar amount before filing as an LLC because they are only thinking about the S corp election. Remember, S corp = tax savings. The S corp election can be made at the same time the LLC is filed, but it doesn't have to be. You can absolutely file the LLC without making the S corp election, which will still give you personal liability protection.

Make sense?

This is why I encourage all of my friends and clients to file for an LLC ASAP. What next? Well, here's a timeline breakdown that should help simplify things for you:

1. File your LLC.
2. Once approved, go to the IRS website to get your employer identification number (EIN). This step is free!
3. Next, take all the documents you received from the IRS regarding your EIN, and those obtained from the state regarding your LLC, and get your business bank account.
4. Then, get your operating agreement in order. Some states also require articles of organization.

You must have a business bank account when you have an LLC. Again, if you mix personal and business funds, you risk losing liability protection. In other words, if you combine your personal and business assets, if your business is ever sued, your personal assets could potentially be on the line. I repeat, do not do this!

How does owning an LLC affect your taxes?

Simple, it doesn't.

As a sole proprietor, when you file your taxes, you file a schedule c on your tax return. Once you file a single-member LLC, you are filing the same thing on your taxes. If your accountant is telling you to wait until you are making money to file your LLC, it's because they are not thinking about your liability. They are only thinking about taxes and the S corp election.

File the LLC and keep yourself and your assets safe. I'm begging you.

Because, look, no one ever plans on getting sued. At least, I hope not. But it happens because we are human beings, and we make mistakes. I don't want that mistake to cost you everything you've ever worked for. Of course, in addition to being an LLC you want insurance, but start with the LLC.

One more time for the people in the back: filing an LLC will not affect your taxes until you make the S corp election. When do you make the S corp election? That is a question for your accountant.

From Sole Proprietor To LLC: When To Make The Change

A question I am constantly asked is — how can I go from sole proprietor to LLC? Well, what if I told you it was so much simpler than you think? To make this change, all you need to do is file as an LLC. Do you need to shut down your sole proprietorship? Well, that depends on a few things.

First, if you are doing business with your social security number and have never filed any documents with your county, state, or anywhere, in this case, you likely don't need to do anything. All you need to do is file the LLC with your state. Now, you can file that alone by going straight into your Secretary of State office. You can also work directly with an attorney or third party like Legalpreneur.

If you work with Legalpreneur, that does not establish a client-attorney relationship. But we will take care of all the legal filings for you and file all the necessary paperwork on your behalf. Filing on your own is the cheapest option, but the decision is entirely yours.

Let's say you decide to file on your own, and have a sole proprietorship that you'd like to turn into an LLC. If you had an EIN for your sole proprietor, it would not work for your LLC. You need a new one! Check with your state and see what else is required. Sometimes it's articles of organization or operating agreements. It just depends on what your state requires.

Considering A Partnership? Here's What To Keep In Mind

First, a quick refresh. A partnership is anytime two or more persons, or other entities contribute money and property to start a business.

A partnership is never subject to federal income taxation, unlike a C corp or S corp. It is not a taxable entity, and the partnership itself is not required to pay taxes. Instead, when it comes to partnerships, the partners are liable for income tax on the taxable income in the partnership. Simple terms – each partner pays taxes on their earnings.

Why would someone want to form a partnership, and when? Great question. For starters, a partnership has more flexibility than a C corp or an S corp. Partnerships can annually allocate income and cash flow between the partners. In contrast, allocation is much more restrictive with a C corp or S corp.

Further, partnerships allow the partners to avoid double taxation and the pooling of resources and have simple filing requirements. Although you do not file federal income tax on the partnership, you are required to file an informational tax return. That's it!

Misunderstood: S Corps And Why I Love Them

An S corp is not a business entity. It's a tax filing status available to certain corporations and LLCs to avoid double taxation.

So what does this mean? And more specifically, what does it mean for you?

Your earnings are subject to double self-employment taxes as a sole proprietor or a single-member LLC. This is because in a traditional 9-5 job, you, the employee, pays 50% of the self-employment taxes. Your employer pays the other 50%. As a self-employed individual, you're the employer and the employee, so you pay double self employment taxes. However, once you make the S corp election, you can pay yourself a reasonable salary, and then what's left over is distributed to you as profit. And the gain is not subject to self-employment taxes. It is passed on to the individual.

In simpler terms, it means that the business itself is exempted from federal corporate income tax. And instead, income from dividends is taxed only at the individual level, based on the marginal income tax rate that applies.

I know some of this may begin to sound confusing. Keep in mind that I'm just trying to give you a high-level overview. Once you make it to this point in business, you should have a certified public accountant (CPA) that can explain exactly how this stuff applies and benefits you.

How is that different from a C corp? Well, for starters, C corp shareholders are not allowed to write off corporate losses to offset other income on personal income statements. Whereas, S corps can avoid double taxation on the corporate level.

To qualify as an S corp, the corporation must:

- Be based in the US
- Have shareholders that meet certain criteria (no partnerships, corporations or non-residents)
- Have only one class of stock
- Have no more than 100 shareholders

If you qualify, you can apply to become an S corp by filing Form 2553 or an Election by a Small Business Corporation document signed by all the shareholders. You can find the form on the IRS website.

P.S., if your business is taxed as an S corp, your business's tax deadline is March 15th!

Taxes and Business Structure

Understanding the nuances in each business structure is crucial to making the right decision. Take the time to carefully review chapter one's checklists to see which business structure best complements your needs. For quick reference, see the tax chart below.

Business Structure	Tax Pros	Tax Cons
Sole Proprietorship	• Pass-through entity • Low cost to set up • No corporate business tax • Minimal reporting requirements	• Unlimited personal liability • Difficult to attain business loans/financing
Partnership	• Pass-through entity • No corporate business taxes • Low cost to set up	• Unlimited personal liability, depending on partnership class
LLC	• Limited personal liability • No corporate business taxes • Flexibility with tax structure	• Not recognized outside of the U.S. • Governed by state statute

C Corporation	• Limited personal liability • Preferred by investors	• Double taxation • Costly • Heavily regulated and requires oversight
S Corporation *Reminder: This isn't an independent entity*	• Pass through entity • Limited liability • No corporate business tax	• Only recognized in the US • Strict qualification standards • Entity must be owned by an individual

Developing A Tax Strategy

The next step is coming up with a plan. Yes, you can expense dinners with your partner, mileage on your car and home decor, but there are guidelines to follow. The purpose of each expense has to be your business, which requires planning.

Here's A List Of Things You *May* Be Able To Write Off:

Expense	Reason
• Camera, props and decor	• Digital marketing
• Weekend trip to Tulum	• Content creation
• Clothing and makeup for a business photoshoot	• Marketing

46

• Dinner with your business partner	• Business meal
• Car expenses (includes fuel, oil changes, parking, repairs, insurance, etc.)	• Transportation
• Internet, rent, office equipment (for those who work from home)	• Home office expenses
• Foreign transaction fees	• Bank transactions, including processing fees are tax deductible.

What's not tax deductible?

Good question. For the most part, things like gym membership fees, commuting costs, labor, fines and penalties. Although that is not an exhaustive list, it gives you a good idea of what things cannot be written off.

**It's important to note, that you should always chat with your tax professional before relying on these deductions. Some may only be applicable to certain businesses.

Tax Tips to Remember

1. **Create A Manageable Structure**

People throw around generic terms like, "you just need a schedule" all the time, without offering any advice on creating, implementing and maintaining that schedule. That's not what I'm going to do to you. Instead, I'll show you exactly how I make tax season a breeze.

- First, give yourself one day every week to collect, organize and file your paperwork. I schedule all my meetings on Mondays and do all my necessary paperwork on Friday afternoons. This gives me Tuesday to Friday mornings to do uninterrupted deep work on my business. Now, of course, this isn't a rigid schedule. Emergencies happen, and it's not like I'd ever ignore a business call because it came in on a Thursday and not Monday. But knowing, more or less, what I'm going to do each day creates a flow that supports the lifestyle I want for myself.
- Fridays are the days that matter most here. All paperwork is on the table, from scheduling my calendar to banking and invoicing. The very first thing I do is go through my transactions for the week. You can only know what you can write off, if you know where your money is going. Once I know what I can write off, I write it in my monthly expense report with the date, amount, and the purpose of the transaction. You

can keep things simple and use an excel spreadsheet for every month, or you can use all-in-one options like QuickBooks. I'll be honest, I love platforms like QuickBooks because they automate so many aspects of business, including invoices and tracking income.

So, that's it. That's literally the system that helps me stay organized when it comes to tax season. Simple right? That's why it works. We are busy people and don't have time to integrate a 10-step process that will take months to get the hang of. If you can commit a few hours weekly to going through your expenses and tracking them, you'll save your business tons of money. You'll also save yourself from the unnecessary stress around tax season.

2. You Don't Need to Hang On To Every Receipt

This one shocks many people. And I think it's one of the reasons why people get overwhelmed with the thought of writing off expenses. Because honestly, who has the time, room or memory to file every single receipt of every business-related transaction? Some old-school tax professionals may tell you it's in your best interest to hold onto everything. But the truth is, you don't have to hold on to the receipts physically. There are many apps available to scan and easily keep track of your receipts. Once it's scanned, you can throw it away!

3. **Pay Estimated Quarterly Taxes**

When you work for an employer, they typically pay your federal and state taxes on your behalf throughout the year. When you are the employer, you need to consider this.

Estimated tax payments are precisely that – your best guess on how much taxes you owe the IRS. These are payments made based on your earnings that are not subject to federal tax withholding. They can include income you've earned from dividends, passive income, freelance revenue and self-employment.

- Who Needs To Be Making These Payments?

The general rule is anyone bringing in income outside of employer and employee relationships.

- Calculating Your Payments

There are a few different ways to calculate what you owe, but the simplest way is to estimate how much you would owe for that year and then divide the total sum by four for each quarter.

Payments are typically due in April, June, September and January each year. Still, check with the IRS website to confirm the exact days.

4. **Hire An Accountant**

This is more of a suggestion than a tip. But please, hire an accountant. I know you can file taxes alone. It's something I did for many years, until my company became an S corp. But I also have a background in accounting. If this is your first year of business, or you are uncomfortable at the thought of filing your own taxes – don't! I can almost guarantee that you're probably paying more taxes than you need to if you are doing it on your own.

5. Consider Getting A Bookkeeper

If you struggle with keeping up with your receipts or expenditures, do yourself the biggest favor and hire a bookkeeper. They will help you stay organized all year round, and it shouldn't cost you more than a few hundred dollars a month.

Business Insurance

Insurance comes in handy in many different situations. Some insurances are highly recommended, while others are required by your state. Typically, there are three types of insurance that may be mandated by your state: workers' compensation insurance, business auto insurance, and disability insurance. Make sure to check your state's requirements because every state is different.

Workers Compensation Insurance
If you have hired employees, you may be required by your state to get workers' compensation insurance. Please check your state website for more specific details on what type of insurance

policy you need. Generally speaking, workers' compensation protects employees if they suffer an injury or disability related to the job. It may also protect your business from potential lawsuits brought by employees or their family members in case of a workplace-related injury.

Business Auto Insurance

Again, this is another instance of state-specific insurance, but it is a requirement. If you have a business car, make sure that the insurance protects both you and anyone who would be driving it. Most companies with cars have an internal policy preventing uninsured passengers from driving the vehicle.

Disability Insurance

This is only required for businesses operating in California, Hawaii, New York, Rhode Island or New Jersey.

Although only these three insurance policies are government-mandated, there are multiple other business-related policies that I would highly recommend considering, depending on your business needs.

Here's a breakdown:

Commercial General Liability (CGL)

CGL is one of the most common types of business insurance. Essentially this insurance protects companies from common lawsuits arising from everyday business activities, including bodily injury, personal injury, and property damage.

Criminal Liability

This insurance will protect your business if an employee intentionally harms a third party or in the case of criminal acts by an employee. You'll want to add this as your team of employees grows.

Errors and Omissions Insurance

If you are a business that handles documents or property belonging to customers, consider getting this insurance. It will protect you in the event that an error or omission by your company causes a loss to the customer. This insurance would cover liability if you forget to include something or make a mistake, which costs your customer.

Product Liability

Product liability protects your business from legal liability in the event that a customer is injured because of your product. This is a very important insurance to consider if you are manufacturing products. You should also develop a risk management plan, that analyzes product safety and risk benefits over the life of the product in question.

Chapter 3:
Contracts

"Always read your contract. Know what you're getting yourself into. Know your worth." — Lil Durk, rapper

Some things in business are non-negotiable, and written contracts are certainly one of them. Think of contracts as an integral part of your business. They are important because they define the rights and duties of all parties to the contract, solidify agreed-upon terms, establish transparency and act as a crucial reference point in times of dispute. It can be easy to talk yourself out of needing a contract – believe me, I've seen it many times. It doesn't matter if you know the person you're going into business with or if they have a stellar reputation. Having a contract protects you financially and legally, and it also elevates the positioning of your business.

The thing is, you can run a business without ever using a contract. Just set up as a sole proprietor and start selling items. Who's going to stop you? If there's one thing you take away from this chapter or even this book, please let it be this: just because you are not legally required to do something, does not mean it's not in your best interest to do so. Let me remind you that it is legal to run a business without doing the things I'm teaching you in this book. However, you have a much higher risk of being sued for not implementing any legal protection within your business. Remember, we're trying to build a wall of protection for our empire.

But it can be tempting. I'd know. It's happened to me. When I owned my clothing boutique, I regularly sent influencers clothing in exchange for content and posting on their page. The trade constituted an implied agreement, and possibly a written contract, because there were conversations had via DM. And even though I wasn't paying them, we entered into a valid contract by giving them clothing in exchange for photos because there was an exchange of value. This is where it gets tricky. It's easy to message an influencer and negotiate work terms. Depending on their popularity and positioning, requiring an additional legal document can seem obsolete. What's the point? They seem professional and do this for a living. But what guarantee do you have that they will hold up their end of the bargain, especially if there is no additional monetary payment? In this instance, having a contract would be an asset. It would highlight and reinforce each party's roles and responsibilities. It would also remind the other party that there's a legally binding contract that they agreed to. I'm not suggesting that you threaten a lawsuit. But contracts carry a certain weight, and simply reminding people about what they agreed to in writing is often sufficient enough to get them to act according to the contract.

Contracts also remind other business owners that you are more than a hobbyist or side hustler and can help you develop invaluable business relationships. If you're still unsure about contracts as a business owner, imagine this. You are an 8-figure business owner and want to go into business with a small retailer. What are some basic expectations you would have? You would likely expect that they were registered as a legal entity, right? *At least, I hope you would.* You'd probably also expect that they formalize any agreement between you in writing. What would you do if a company suggested going into business with you and decided to waive contract requirements? It would seem strange, unprofessional and off-putting. But as much as contracts protect you legally, they also protect you from looking like an amateur.

I'm not here to say you should sue someone every time an issue occurs in a contract. Lawsuits are costly and very stressful. However, if you do have a written contract, many states will allow you to collect treble damages and attorney fees if you have to sue to collect payment. The pure fact that you're eligible for these damages could highly motivate someone that has refused to pay according to the contract schedule. So what are treble damages?

They are state-specific damages, where the amount of actual damage is calculated and multiplied by three. If your actual damages are $10,000, you could walk away with $30,000 in treble damages alone. In most states, you can only sue someone for two types of damages – punitive damages and compensatory damages. Punitive damages are meant to act as a punishment for the defendant, and deter them from doing shady business. So, if you're suing someone for not finishing a website after paying them, punitive damages would exceed the amount you paid them to complete the project. Conversely, compensatory damages are intended to compensate you for your loss. It will put you in the position you would have been in had the contract never existed in the first place. Think of this as the refund damages.

Now, while these are the damages the courts can award you, there are also the damages you can put in your contract. For example, if you are a service-based business and deal with invoicing, you can add a penalty for late payment directly into the contract. There's nothing more frustrating than chasing payment, and you shouldn't have to. Instead, put late payment penalties in your contracts to encourage prompt payment.

But what if I trust the person I'm going into business with?

I hear you. An existing relationship can often make contracts seem like an unnecessary formality. But believe me, they are just as crucial between friends, if not more so. In addition to outlining rights and responsibilities, contracts also finalize the agreed-upon terms. They keep tabs to ensure that what you agreed to six months ago is what you deliver, not what you interpreted further down the road.

What Makes A Contract?

Contracts are relatively easy to draft, and the truth is, you don't always need to hire a lawyer to prepare one for you. In legalese, to have a valid contract, there must be an offer, acceptance, consideration and a mutual understanding between all involved parties that there is intent to be bound. In clearer terms, this indicates that a contract is formed when one party accepts an offer made by the other party, if there is an exchange of value (consideration). The parties intend to be bound to the terms of the agreement.

Here's a step-by-step guide on how to draft your own contract:

1. At the top of the page, write down the names of the parties and their respective roles. The purpose here is to make the parties easily identifiable.
2. Next, describe what the agreement pertains to. What service or product is being contracted? Be explicit about expectations, deliverables, and the personalized details integral to the agreement.
3. Decide the length of the agreement. Is this a monthly retainer with ongoing work? Is there an agreed upon delivery date?
4. Payment. Not just the amount, but when will payment be made? How will it be made?

5. Highlight potential consequences of breaching the agreement. What are the penalties for non-delivery or non-payment?
6. Can the contract be terminated early? What happens if it is terminated early?
7. Determine how the parties will resolve the conflict. What state laws will govern? Will the conflict be resolved through dispute resolution alternatives, such as mediation or arbitration?
8. The final step is signing and dating your document. In many instances, a contract must be signed by both parties to be enforceable.

Of course, there are additional clauses that your contract may need. Unfortunately, most business owners won't know what specific clauses or contracts their company needs until it's too late. That's why I suggest getting started with attorney-drafted contract templates, like the ones drafted by Legalpreneur in The Contract Vault, rather than attempting to prepare your own. A template can be found through a quick google search, but remember that many of these contracts will be beyond the scope of your business. And you can get pretty lost in the sauce looking at contract templates, whether you are a budding or seasoned entrepreneur. Often, templates will include convoluted legal terms and clauses that even the best lawyer would be hard-pressed to define accurately. In The Contract Vault, you'll find succinct templates covering all of your business needs. We currently have over 100 templates in

The Contract Vault for various industries.

Here's a sample of what's inside:

- Affiliate Agreement
- Anti-Retaliation Policy
- Assignment of Rights
- Brand Representative Agreement
- Breathwork Client Agreement
- Business Partnership Agreement
- Cancellation of Services
- Cease and Desist Letter
- Client Testimonial Release
- Co-Creation Agreement
- Coaching Agreement
- Confidentiality Agreement
- Course Terms
- COVID-19 Waiver
- Credit Card Authorization Form
- Design Contract (Florist)
- Disclaimers
- Employee Agreement
- Employee Termination Letter
- Engagement Contract (Photography)
- Engagement Letter (Accounting)
- Event Sponsorship Agreement
- Fitness Waiver Template
- General License Agreement

- Guest Blog Post Agreement
- HIPAA Acknowledgement and Consent
- HIPAA Business Associate Agreement
- Independent Contractor Agreement
- Influencer Agreement
- Master Services Agreement
- Mastermind Agreement
- Media Release Form
- Medical Questionnaire
- Model Release Form
- Non-Compete and Non-Solicitation Agreement
- Non-Disclosure Agreement
- Non-Disclosure, Non-Circumvention and Non-Competition Agreement
- Office Lease Agreement
- Operating Agreement Template
- Party Rental Agreement
- Photography Agreement
- Photography License
- Podcast Co-Host Agreement
- Podcast Guest Consent Form
- Podcast Sponsorship Agreement
- Privacy Policy
- Product Design Contract
- Release of Information (Health-Wellness)
- Rental Agreement (Event Space)
- Rescheduling Agreement (Florist)
- Right to Publicity License

- Sales Representative Agreement
- Services Agreement (Bookkeeping)
- Speaker Contract
- Terms and Conditions
- Terms of Use
- Volunteer Agreement and Release From Liability
- Wholesale Agreement
- Nondisclosure Agreement (Contractor)
- Rescheduling Agreement
- Services Agreement

I found that business owners were coming to me in my law firm to draft custom contracts for them and their new businesses. Because they hadn't been in business very long, the client didn't know what they needed in their contract. And that's absolutely okay. I don't expect you to know the ins and outs of business contracts. But the thing is, if you don't recognize what you need, you'll end up paying for things that don't apply to you. I wanted to streamline this process and save business owners as much money as I could, so I launched The Contract Vault.

There are so many times in your business when you are going to want to use a contract. When I put together The Contract Vault, it was because I didn't want entrepreneurs to feel overwhelmed when it came to protecting their business. These pre-drafted contracts are the easiest and most efficient way to protect your business without drowning yourself in paperwork and never-ending legal fees. Because I'd rather you put your money elsewhere.

Bear in mind, these contracts probably won't get you through your entire business career. They're meant to be a great starting point with industry best practices. Eventually, you'll learn what you do and don't want in your contracts, and graduate to custom contracts. But for now, this is a great place to start.

What Happens When You Don't Have A Contract?

If you did not memorialize your agreement in a single document, all is not lost. You may still have an enforceable contract, either via oral agreement or if you can show through emails, texts, and other documents that you and the other party intended to be bound to agreed-upon terms. However, many times it's costly to prove these types of contracts exist, and it's pricey to enforce them.

Contract Clauses To Look Out For

There's a lot of flexibility in drafting a valid contract. But that doesn't mean there aren't things you should watch out for.

Orally Agreed Upon Terms
First, if you have a written agreement, you want to ensure that **everything** is in the final contract. Oral agreements can still be valid contracts. However, enforcing terms agreed upon orally becomes significantly more challenging if there's also a written

agreement. Typically, once there is a written agreement, all arrangements made before the physical contract are null and void. That's why you need to "always get it in writing!"

Yes, there are ways of arguing that oral statements made prior to or contemporaneous with the written document are valid. However, it's an obstacle you should attempt to avoid.

Convoluted Terms

Make sure that you understand what you agree to. Contracts can be long, confusing and unnecessarily wordy. Although a contract's validity requires both parties to agree, in some cases, you can be signing away rights you shouldn't be or don't need to. In such an instance, you are responsible for educating yourself on the meanings of the terms you're agreeing to. The solution? Don't sign anything you do not understand.

The other solution is joining the Legalpreneur Membership, which includes a complimentary document review by a licensed attorney. You shouldn't be expected to sign a document you don't understand, and now you don't have to.

Penalties

Always be sure to see if there's a damages clause outlined in the agreement. If something goes wrong, are you okay with the penalties? Do you have a grace period that would allow you to "cure" or fix the error? Although there may be a due date for the payment, is there also a stated late fee? That due date could be irrelevant if there's no late penalty. If that's important to you, speak up before it's formalized in writing.

Ownership of Work

Perhaps this may be a more specific red flag. But, if you are signing an independent contractor agreement, or providing a service to a client, check to see who owns the rights to the work product and the restrictions. This is one of the most important contract clauses for small business owners. Just because you pay someone to create something for you doesn't mean you own that final work product. It could mean you only have a license (permission) to use the work for a limited time.

Intellectual Property Clause **Typically, this is the most important clause in a contract!

Creatives and content creators, pay attention to the intellectual property clause! This clause is similar to ownership of work but slightly different. The intellectual property clause essentially allocates ownership or rights to potential creations that arise from a business relationship. You typically find IP clauses in employment contracts, service agreements, consultancy agreements, joint ventures, and co-development agreements. If your intellectual property is important to you, ensure you retain rights to the knowledge and information you bring into the partnership, or negotiate a rate that adequately compensates you for your intangible assets. One of the most common examples I see is with brand collaborations. You may be creating content as an influencer to promote a brand on your own page, or you might be a UGC creator that is creating content for the brand to use for their purposes. In any event, by default, you, the creator, own the intellectual property of that content. However, most brands will want to own this content. That's fine if you're okay with it, but I highly suggest charging accordingly to transfer ownership rights to the brand.

Non-Compete Clauses

Listen, I understand why you'd want to use one of these in your contract. But I have some bad news. Non-compete clauses are rarely enforceable because they limit a person's ability to earn a living. So what is the solution if you want to ensure that an employee doesn't compete with your business after leaving your company?

A confidentiality agreement! The accord will ensure that your intellectual property and tricks of the trade stay within your company after the employee has parted ways. You can also apply this to independent contractors.

Non-Disparagement Clause

A non-disparagement agreement is a clause in a contract where the signing party agrees not to speak negatively about the company in any form of communication. Typically between employer and employee it can also apply to independent contractors and clients.

What Contracts Are Needed In Your Business?

For the most part, I tell business owners to use a contract whenever money changes hands. But there's more than that. I've laid out a few of the most common contracts below.

Privacy Policy

A privacy policy is required by law to be on every website. If you don't have a privacy policy on your website, it's not in compliance. The privacy policy covers what personal information you gather from website visitors, how you will use that information and whether you may sell to third parties. If it sounds like it's over your head and not something you want to draft on your own, don't worry because it's in The Contract Vault!

Terms of Use

This contract stands as the agreement between you and the website's visitors. It may not sound familiar to have a contract with a website visitor but trust me—you want this on your website. This can also double as the terms of purchase if users can purchase something from your website.

Service Agreement

If you are a service provider, this is the contract between you and your clients. This contract is probably the most important one in your business when you're a service provider. So make sure you're always very clear about what's included in the agreement between you and your client.

Independent Contractor Agreement

If you're hiring someone to do a project for you, it's probably best to bring them on as an independent contractor instead of an employee. As you can imagine, this contract governs the relationship between you and the contractor. Therefore, it will be a pretty common contract you use in your business, and it may not always have this name.

Employee Agreement

When you do hire actual W2 employees, you want to ensure that there is absolutely a written agreement. It can double as the employee handbook, but it can also be separate. In the employee agreement, it's imperative to lay out the standards for employment, benefits, time off policy, etc.

How To Sign Contracts

It may seem silly to have a paragraph in this book about how to sign contracts. But there are multiple ways to sign them, and I want to make certain you always have them properly signed.

The good ol' fashioned way is to sign the contracts with a pen in person. In today's digital world, signing contracts in person is not always feasible. You can also email the document to have the other party print, sign, scan and send it back. Funny enough, I feel like that's pretty old school these days.

My favorite option is using a digital signature service such as HelloSign or DocuSign. We will also be implementing our own signature service to the MyLegalpreneur app very soon. Digital signatures are my favorite option because of the audit trails and the fact that the contract can't be completed until all fields are filled.

I once had a client who emailed the contract to her new client, who printed out the contract, signed it, and then sent it back to my client. It wasn't until a few months later, after the relationship went sour, that my client realized the other party didn't sign the contract properly. Specifically, there were two places for a signature and they only signed one spot. Although not the end of the world, it made my client's case for losing $10,000 a slam dunk. That's why the digital signature options are my favorite.

The other option is checking the box. We've all seen it. We go to purchase something online, and just before confirming the purchase, we mark the box that says, "By checking the box, I agree to the Terms and Conditions." It is legally binding if the box is not already checked, and the terms and conditions are clickable to go read on another page.

I do get many questions about whether a client should also get a signature on top of checking the box. Like I said above, checking the box is perfectly legal, but we're not just talking about legalities here. We want to lower your risk level. And when it comes to chargebacks, a signed contract is your best friend. So even though it's legally binding to check the box, you're more likely to win a chargeback when there's a signed contract instead of just showing a checkbox.

When Can A Business Forgo Using A Contract?

There's always an exception. Yes, contracts are critically important, but there are limits. In some instances, it's okay to skip a written contract. Here are a few examples:

- *In-person fitness classes:* If you're hosting a pop-up fitness class, there's not necessarily a need to have attendees sign a 20-page contract each time before the class. If there's a membership at the gym where you're teaching the fitness classes, then there's typically a contract that should cover the classes. I recommend having them sign a waiver to ensure you're not responsible if they hurt themselves during these classes.
- *Podcast guest consent forms:* Every time I go on as a guest on someone's podcast, I do not want to read a 10-page-long contract. Your podcast guests do not need to sign these huge contracts to come on an episode. Again, what you do need for guests on your podcast are clearly laid out terms! If you're using a scheduler to line up your podcast guests, such as Calendly, lay out the terms in the description where they schedule. That way they will read and agree to the terms when they sign up for the guest episode. Terms included in the contract may

be: the right to use their likeness, the right to repurpose the content, the use of headphones and a microphone, etc. As long as you have the essential terms presented to them, it's legally binding! You don't need a full-blown written contract, but you do need terms.

When To Hire A Lawyer

One of the reasons people shy away from using contracts is that they overcomplicate the process.

It feels like plagiarism to download a contract off Google, slap your company name on it, and consider it a legal document. But not everything is meant to be complicated, and that contract you downloaded is a legal document. The issue is whether each clause pertains to the actual agreement at hand.

The other reason people choose to avoid implementing contracts is because they believe an excellent contract requires hiring a lawyer and paying hefty legal fees. But that couldn't be further from the truth. Consider hiring a lawyer when your business is ready for specific and personalized contractual agreements. For example, if you have specific intellectual property rights that you want to retain or a manufacturing agreement that requires unique language, then you may need a lawyer to draft a custom contract. If your business is just getting off the ground, it may be best to start with templates. However, if you're not sure and want the peace of mind knowing you hired a lawyer to make sure your ducks are in a row, then go ahead!

Step By Step If A Client Doesn't Pay Or Perform

Here are a series of potential actions to take if someone doesn't do what they're supposed to. Of course, feel free to eliminate what doesn't apply to your situation.

1. Send a friendly email reminding them of what they need to do.
2. Send an email checking in since you haven't heard from them (assuming they never responded).
3. Send an email with the signed contract reminding them that they signed the contract and point them to the sections they have breached. If you're a Legalpreneur Member, I usually suggest cc'ing your attorney at this point to signal you legitimately have an attorney and will get them involved if it's needed. **This type of email typically has a 95% success rate.
4. Send a demand letter from your attorney. This action will cost money. I've seen rates anywhere from $300 to upwards of $1000.
5. File a lawsuit depending on how much is owed or what needs to be completed. Check your local state laws on whether you should file in a small claims court or a different court.

For more resources and templates, go to https://thelegalpreneur.com/legalpreneurbook-resources/

Chapter 4: Collecting and Protecting the $$$

"I hereby break all contracts I made unconsciously and consciously before I knew the depth of my own spirit; the silent ones, the ones I inherited, passed down and accepted as my own from generation to generation."

— Andrea Sager

You're in business to turn a profit. Yes, there's passion and the power of being your own boss, but ultimately, what makes a business a business is the fact that it's profit-driven. That means at each stage of running your company, you need to make strategic decisions to ensure that your investments, decisions and business plan are what's best for your bottom line. It's a game of simultaneously balancing short-term and long-term benefits to build a company with longevity and a healthy return on investment.

Before your business can welcome clients, you need to decide on a payment service provider. If you've shopped online, you've used one before. A payment service provider is a third-party company that helps businesses process and accept a wide range of online payment methods, including credit cards, debit cards, and more. There are many reasons for why you need to be careful in deciding on which service provider to utilize. Here are some factors you should consider when choosing a service provider:

1. **The Provider's Reputation**

Research each service provider and find out what other businesses have to say. A quick google search can do wonders in helping you decide if a provider is right for you. The provider's reputation will also go a long way with your clients. Put yourself in their position – would you give your card information to a website that used a questionable service provider? There are certain symbols or logos that we look for when deciding whether to purchase online, and there's a reason for that – it creates trust. When it comes to business expenses, choosing a reputable service provider is not an area you will want to cut corners on for financial sake. Choosing to do so can hurt your bottom line, credibility and future of your brand. Be smart, strategic and play the long game.

2. **Cost And Offerings**

In researching the cost of the service, check to see how you are being charged. Is it per transaction? Is it a flat fee? And does the amount change depending on how much you sell? You need to ask yourself these questions when deciding which provider you can afford. Be sure to ask what the service costs are, and what's included in that cost to ensure that you are getting the best possible deal for your company. If possible, do cost modeling with different providers to determine who would cost the least. Without realizing how much costs can impact your bottom line, you can easily find yourself spending 5-10 times more than you should on processing fees.

3. Business Capacity

Look at the types of businesses the service provider typically works with. Can they handle your business needs? Compare their existing clients to what your needs are, and ask questions. For example, what types of businesses do they typically work with? If you're an online business coach and they normally only work with local brick and mortar businesses, it's probably not a good fit for either of you. You'll want to understand this before making your decision.

4. Chargeback Protection

It is essential to choose a provider that is an expert in their field and has a track record of handling typical problems that arise in a financial transaction. For example, one of the biggest issues and pain points for small businesses is chargebacks. They occur when a customer files a complaint with their service provider and disputes a transaction as fraudulent or incomplete. In many cases, the customer is given a refund by the service provider, leaving you, the business owner, at a loss.

Understanding Your Options

Some commonly used providers are Paypal, Stripe, Square, Apple Pay, Shopify, and Square Payments. That list is not exhaustive, but don't overwhelm yourself by looking at the pros and cons of every single possibility. Instead, look at what's commonly used in your industry and by similarly situated businesses. There's a reason the providers I listed above are popular – but that doesn't mean they are perfect—far from it.

When clients ask me which payment service provider they should utilize, my response often depends on what they offer as a business. For example, if you are a service-based business, PayPal is not your friend. Here's why.

I once had a client lose $18,000. She had been hired to build an extravagant custom website for a company and she accepted payment through PayPal (this was before she knew I existed!). She built the website to the client's specifications, and the transaction was completed, until it wasn't. One day, my client checked her online banking account, only to see she was missing $18,000. The company that hired her started a dispute on PayPal, claiming they did not receive the website. Although we worked together to refute their claims, and show that she had in fact developed the website and submitted it to the company by their requested deadline, it didn't get her her money back. She lost $18,000, and the client received the website and the refund.

How did this happen?

For starters, PayPal was created for product-based businesses. It continues to operate in that way. When someone disputes a transaction on PayPal, the seller has the opportunity to refute the claim, typically by providing a confirmation of shipment, a written contract, or any other items that will prove that what was paid for was delivered. It is possible to win a claim with PayPal. However, if the customer then goes directly to the credit card company, the credit card company will take the money from PayPal, and PayPal will take that money from you. Yes, even if you already won a claim with PayPal. So why do so many service-based businesses continue to use it? That I'm not sure of. I can only presume it's because they don't know any better. My client lost $18,000 because of PayPal's chargeback system. They initially won the dispute with PayPal. However, the company that hired her went above PayPal and straight to her credit card company. The credit card company took the money from PayPal, and PayPal got the money from my client. There's nothing my client could have done to win with PayPal. Of course, this only becomes an issue when there's a disputed transaction. But why take the risk?

When you are looking for a payment service provider, make sure to ask yourself the following questions:

1. Can the eCommerce payment flow scale effortlessly as your business grows?
2. Is the payment gateway provider certified?
3. Does the payment gateway provider follow security standards?
4. How much will you be paying in service fees?
5. Are the costs to be paid per month, per transaction, or both?
6. What is the provider's chargeback policy?
7. Is there a set-up fee?
8. Is there a monthly fee to use the service?
9. Are there service agreement requirements? If so, what does it entail?
10. How efficient will the transaction be for the customer? Will they have to register for an account?
11. Is the payment service provider easy to use on mobile devices, and desktops?
12. What is the integration process like?
13. What is customer service like? Is there 24-hour support for users and merchants?
14. Will the provider charge more for international cards?
15. Is there a minimum limit for usage?
16. If your business does "launches" and has high revenue every few months, you need to find out if they will hold the funds for an extended period of time during the launches.

Now, on the flip side, I have a client who uses PayPal religiously. She makes roughly $20,000 monthly from a $10/month subscription service. Even if she were to experience 10% in chargebacks each month (highly unlikely), that's $100/month she's losing. For her, the low cost of her product makes the pros of using PayPal worth the risk. Using PayPal is not necessarily a no-go. I want to make sure you understand the risks before doing so.

Here's a brief breakdown of some of the most common payment processors and when you would want to use them.

1. PayPal is one of the most widely used payment processors, but it's not without risks. I typically advise that clients stay away from using PayPal. Still, as I mentioned above, it is a personal choice. PayPal also offers Buy Now, Pay Later, which makes it an attractive option for shoppers. It's reputable, easy to use, and convenient, so it's no surprise that it's an option so many businesses use. If you know and understand the risks, I say go for it if you're a product-based business.

2. Shopify Payments is a great all-in-one option for businesses that use Shopify for their e-commerce. I love how Shopify integrates all the standard payment processing a business owner would need. It includes credit cards, debit cards, mobile wallets, and even cryptocurrency. They also offer great support when it

comes to credit card chargebacks. Now, you don't have to use Shopify's payment processor if you are using the Shopify platform. But in some instances, it may be your best option. Back when I used to have my online clothing boutique, I did use Shopify payments, and it worked seamlessly.

3. Square is another much-loved payment processor best known for its in-person transaction services. When you set up a Square account, you will get a Square Reader, which is a cute little card reader that attaches itself right to your phone. The latest version of the Square Reader allows tap-to-pay mobile wallet transactions. It gets even better, though. Square has one of the lowest fees of major payment processors.

4. Stripe is best known for the wide range of payment options they offer. As a business owner, you can implement Stripe's API on your existing website to allow customers to use numerous payment methods, including the following: Apple Pay, Google Pay, Alipay, Buy-Now-Pay-Later, credit cards and debit cards.

5. Clover feels like a best-kept secret, and I'm really not sure why! This payment processor was designed with in-person transactions in mind. While it's similar to Square in some ways, there are distinct differences. Clover allows you to accept payments from multiple

platforms, including Venmo! See why it's a great option for in-person payments?

6. You may never have used QuickBooks before, but you've surely heard of it. It's one of the most popular software programs for small businesses, and with good reason. Think about it as a one-stop shop for managing your business's financial health. It supports you in invoicing clients, paying bills, preparing taxes, and generating financial reports. What I love about QuickBooks is that it simplifies getting paid. There's nothing more frustrating than chasing down unpaid invoices, with QuickBooks, you don't have to. You can set automatic reminders, request payment, and keep track of how many outstanding balances you have.

   If you're a company that deals with sending invoices, it may be worthwhile to invest in a QuickBooks subscription. It will smooth out your operations, and be a big asset during tax time. The downside of QuickBooks is that the fees are higher than most of the other options above.

Each payment processor has its own little formula for how transactional fees are calculated. Typically the charge is anywhere from 2.5% to 2.9%, plus an additional base fee per transaction. When it comes to deciding what payment processor to use, check out what people in your industry are using and look for their reasoning. If you are in a profession that has a higher risk of chargebacks, you will want to factor that into your decision-making. After that, honestly kick it old school, pull out your favorite notebook and make a to-do list. It comes down to what works best for you and your company.

But wait. One more payment service provider is joining the ranks, and it may be the best one yet.

Introducing Legalpreneur Payments

Coming soon for Legalpreneur Members, Legalpreneur Payments is aimed at lowering costs and providing chargeback protection. Even if you lose the chargeback, Legalpreneur will reimburse you for the lost payment.

Get on the waitlist to be the first to hear about Legalpreneur Payments.

thelegalpreneur.com/payments

How To Offer Payment Plans

If you are a service provider with higher price points, it may be tempting to offer a payment plan for the convenience of your clients. Some people refuse to offer payment plans. That's completely fine, but let me share my story of offering payment plans and why I think it's a good idea.

When I started my law firm, I knew I wanted to be affordable to small business owners. My primary service was trademark filings, which were $1500-$2000. I remember running the idea of a payment plan by a few other trademark attorneys, and they were completely against it. They had it in their head that they would get stiffed by clients. Taking it back to the mindset from chapter 1, I simply was not available to that energy. I saw the small business owners that deeply desired to protect their businesses. But they didn't always have an extra $1500-$2000 available to protect their business name. I began offering payment plans for up to 3 months, which was the best decision I could have ever made. Those 3-month payment plans contributed to almost $500,000 in revenue. Out of all of those clients, only one didn't finish making their payments. That specific client ended up going out of business, and I didn't pursue her for the balance. Instead, I ate the cost. Some days I'm still amazed at how great the payment plans did.

It's important to note that I did these payment plans independently. We set up the payments for each client to run each month automatically. Yes, there were times when payments failed, and all but one client provided a new payment method. If you're interested in offering payment plans, you can also run them on your own. However, you also have other options.

By now, you've probably heard of Affirm, Afterpay, Sezzle and Klarna. For what it's worth, I think they are great. No matter the price point of your products, utilizing one of these services will make your offerings more accessible. One of my favorite things about the pay-later apps currently on the market is the diversity. Each app caters to a different social group, including students, those without credit, and those with bad credit.

According to Investopedia, here's a list of the best pay-later apps currently on the market:

Best Overall: Affirm
Best for Flexible Payment Plans: Sezzle
Best for Students: Afterpay
Best for No Credit Check: Splitit
Best for Bad Credit: Perpay
Best for Small Purchases: PayPal Pay in 4
Best for Large Purchases: Klarna

How do the apps work? Typically, as the merchant, you'll pay a small transaction fee each time someone utilizes the pay-later app. You can always recover the amount by slightly increasing each payment to cover the transaction cost. Some of these options are only for specific industries, so do your research!

When To Call A Collection Agency

Raise your hand if you've had a client sign up for a payment plan and ghost before all payments have been completed. It happens, and unfortunately, it can be a hard thing to prevent. Of course, you want to be a compassionate business owner. We all go through financial hardships; sometimes, the hiccup is out of their control. However, as a business owner, you still have bills to pay.

You can follow the steps at the end of this chapter to try and get the payment. One other option is if the customer does not respond or pay, then reach out again, outlining your intentions to hand over the claim to a collection agency.

It's in your company's best interest to only hire a collection agency as a last resort. There's a few reasons for that. Namely, it's a costly expense with no guarantees and will likely ruin your relationship with the client. Of course, there's an exception to everything. My general rule of thumb is to call a collection agency only when you have exhausted all other options and it's been months since the customer's last payment.

The Ideal Refund Policy

You've probably considered your refund policy if you are a product-based business or someone who offers refunds on their services. And what you decide, is entirely up to you.

However, I believe it's in your best interest to have a policy that states "no refunds." In fact, I think you should expressly put in your contract that your product and services are nonrefundable. The reason? Because you can easily go back and make an exception on a case-by-case basis. But by default, you don't want to allow for automatic refunds. If your contract states that refunds are granted on a case-by-case basis, you will 100% have people that will hound you until you give them a refund.

I've had a few clients who've had to deal with nightmare refund requests. One, in particular, stands out to me. Her client had asked her for a $7,500 refund for a service. For context, my client runs an ad agency, She went above and beyond in getting her clients ads out into the world. She did everything she was supposed to within her contract. However, the client was still unhappy with the return on investment.

There are many industries and professions where results cannot be guaranteed. Ad agencies are one of them. So, of course, when my team and I draft these contracts, the only thing my client is obligated to do is deliver the ads. We make sure to include a clause that expressly says results are not guaranteed. When her client requested a refund, the ad agency owner had already completed over 75% of her obligations.

How would you respond in that situation?

If your knee-jerk reaction is to fold and give in to your client's demands, ask yourself why that is. Is it perfectionist tendencies? Do you worry about your client bad-mouthing you? Or do you not feel entitled to compensation for work you've already done? I need you to remember this: you are worthy of success. Enough with the imposter syndrome, or letting yourself believe that you are doing a terrible job because someone isn't happy with your work. You still did the labor, and that deserves compensation.

When I had my law firm, I often found myself tempted to provide client's a refund when I didn't achieve the desired result they wanted. I had to work on myself to realize that results are not guaranteed, and I'm still worthy of getting paid even if the client was not happy with the results. If you find yourself in this position, ask yourself what the contract is for. For instance, if you're promising results, then a refund would probably be warranted if the results weren't achieved. But most of the time, you're not reassuring results, and if that's the case, you don't need to provide a refund.

Many of us tend to be people pleasers because it's how we learned to earn love from our caregivers. As women, many of us are also socialized to do everything possible to keep those around us happy. But who does that serve? Certainly not your pockets or bottom line.

When dealing with a problematic client, give yourself a moment to pause and recenter. You can do hard things, and running a business can teach you that if you let it. Permit yourself to practice setting boundaries for how you treat yourself and how others treat you.

P.S. Can you guess what advice I gave my client?

You better believe I told her to stand her ground. Had she cut corners and not delivered the services she had contractually agreed to, our conversation would have looked a lot different.

But she can't control what is beyond her, and I ensured that was in her contract before she onboarded this client.

Then the client threatened to give her bad reviews and ruin her reputation. In other words, she tried to bully my client into getting her way.

See what I mean about our trauma and triggers showing up in our business? I see this happening all the time. Then they took it one step further and threatened to get a lawyer involved and sue. Because my client was a Legalpreneur client, I told her to Cc me as a legal backup. Want to know what happened next? Her client backed down almost immediately. They were trying to scare my client into taking action, but they didn't have legal grounds for a lawsuit and knew it.

I had a similar experience with another client who owns a book-writing agency. In this case, my client was working with someone who had not put in the required work. But instead of taking accountability for her lack of action, she asked my client for a refund. He reached out to me immediately after to ask what his options were.

His gut knew she did not deserve a refund. But he still doubted whether or not he was in the right. Think of it this way – every time you offer someone an unwarranted refund on your work, you subconsciously tell your mind that your labor is not worthy. Think about it. Contracts are in place to bind you to something. You are making a commitment. Leniency to break that commitment should not be given out freely.

The Power Of Organization

The key to getting paid and staying paid is organization. Think about it. How many bad business decisions come from not having all the information, or misplacing valuable documents. Take the time to create systems that work not just for your business but for you as a person. You can have all the platforms and software programs your favorite business savvy content creators are raving about. But if it doesn't work for you, does it matter? Same when it comes to payment processors. Getting organized, staying on top of things and making insightful decisions is the best way to build a sustainable business with a solid foundation.

For more resources and templates, go to https://thelegalpreneur. com/legalpreneurbook-resources/

Chapter 5:
The Power of Trademarks

"Whether you realize it or not, intellectual property is your business's most valuable asset." — *Andrea Sager*

There are three main areas of intellectual property law: trademark law, copyright law and patent law. Although they function similarly, each area of law is distinct in its requirements, what it protects and how it's applied.

Trademarks apply to elements of your brand's identity, whereas copyright protects original expression and patents protect inventions. It's possible to utilize each aspect of intellectual property (IP) law to protect your company, but before you can do that, you need to understand how each area functions individually.

Throughout this chapter, we'll focus primarily on trademark law, but in upcoming chapters, we'll discuss copyright and patent law. Understanding how each area of law can potentially fit within your business is crucial. Your intellectual property can become a lucrative business asset if utilized correctly. And that's what I'm here to help you do.

In 2018, I started my law firm, Andrea Sager Law PLLC. Within two years, I had made a million dollars, and about 80% of my work was from trademarks. I quickly learned how vital trademarks are in my legal and business career. I then transferred that into educating others on how essential trademarks are, especially for online business owners. That's why I'm so passionate about trademarks. Perhaps it's why this is my favorite chapter of the whole book. So, let's get to it!

First, What's A Trademark?

Think of a trademark as your business signature. It's a mark, symbol, or word legally registered and used to represent or identify your company or an element of your company. Essentially, this is how the public perceives your brand, product, or service. According to the United States Patent and Trademark Office (USPTO), it can be any word, phrase, symbol, or design individually or in combination. For example, is there a phrase that you always use or a logo that goes on all your products? What about a unique name for your product or service? What do people think of when they think of your brand? These are elements you'd likely want to trademark and capitalize off of.

Common Law vs Federal Trademark

There's good news, and there's bad news. The good news is that you may be eligible for trademark protection even if you didn't register your trademark. The bad news is that safeguard may not be as expansive as you'd like.

Common law trademarks protect symbols, logos, product name, or other words or marks that identify the source of goods or services **before** it is registered with the state or federally. As a local business owner, common law protection is a great way to protect your intellectual property because it gives you an avenue to stop local competitors from using your mark. But that's where it ends. It has regional restrictions that would make it next-to-impossible to enforce outside the state and beyond.

How do you get your mark protected under a common law trademark? It's pretty easy. All you need to do is use it in commerce in a specific geographic area. Unlike federal trademarks, which give you protection throughout the United States, no application is required nor are there any associated fees. But I don't want you to think this is what you should aim for regarding trademark protection. I always encourage my clients to take the extra steps and file a federal trademark application. Trust me, the benefits of having a federal trademark registration outweigh the cost and time associated with the application process. The only time I'd recommend saving your pennies and sticking with common law trademarks is when you run a very niche business. All your customers come from a specific geographic area, and you aren't eligible for federal protection. But if you have online sales or clients beyond your region, stick to filing a federal trademark.

Remember, federal protection is always better than common law protection. The latter is something to keep in mind when you aren't eligible for federal protection, and may have infringers.

So what are these geographic restrictions, and what does that even mean?

Here's an example to help you make sense of things. You open up a stationary store in Texas that has become well-known, and you are happily selling the best pens and paper that money can buy. Common law rights will protect your trademark rights in this case and will prevent any other stationary store from opening around you under the same or a similar name. Why is that? Well, because it's not fair. You've built a brand and have regional recognition. People buy your pens because they expect a certain quality because of the reputation you've created. Allowing someone else to "steal your thunder" would violate unfair competition statutes and state trademark laws.

But what if a stationary store wanted to operate in Nevada or New Mexico under the same or similar name? Sure, it won't financially impact your physical store. Shoppers from New

Mexico wouldn't necessarily drive all the way over to Texas whenever they wanted to go to a stationary store. But can it impact your online presence? Absolutely! Especially when it comes to your social media footprint and e-commerce. Brand confusion can be detrimental to your brand's reputation, so if growing in the digital space matters to you, definitely file for federal trademark protection.

Is it making sense so far? I hope so!

P.S., you can always find more on trademarks on my blog, podcast, or social media pages. Check the resource section of the book for more details.

Now, back to federal trademarks.

Typically, when people think about trademarks, they think about that little ® sign next to a logo or brand name. Remember this: that only comes with a federal trademark registration. It doesn't apply to common law. So even if you toss it up on your logo, it means zilch, nada, absolutely nothing. Once you have a federal registration, you have the exclusive right to use the mark with the goods or services you claimed on your application, and you can now use the ®.

On the other hand, if you want to use the ™ symbol, you can. It only means that you claim to have the exclusive right to use the mark. It does not mean you have the exclusive right to use that mark. Only the ® symbol means you have the exclusive right to use the mark. So don't try to be slick and use the ® symbol without having a federal registration. It's fraud, and you can get in a lot of trouble.

Here's a quick breakdown of some benefits that come with a federal trademark:

- *National protection*

Whereas state registration covers only the state and common law only covers a specific regional area, federal registration will provide you with national coverage. If you plan on scaling your business, either digitally or physically, and hope to do business outside of your home state, then I definitely suggest taking the time to file a federal trademark application.

- *Notice of ownership*

When you file for a federal trademark, it appears on the United States Patent and Trademark office's online trademark database. It's a searchable database that's accessible to the general public. This allows people with similar marks to look up what's been filed and what's protected, before filing their own application. Even just having an application on the website and not yet being registered tends to deter others from using the same or a similar name.

- *More likely to win an infringement case in court*

If someone infringes on your trademark, having a federal

registration gives you an advantage because you're able to bring the case to federal court, and you have the presumption of validity. So if your case ever goes to trial, it's assumed that the other party infringed, and the burden is placed on them to show that they didn't. Federal registration also allows you to pursue statutory damages, which means that you don't actually have to show that you incurred a financial loss to get money from the opposing party. If you win your claim, the amount is pre-determined by statute. Basically, you have a huge advantage in court.

- *Protection against imports of similar brands*

They say imitation is the biggest form of flattery, but that's not always true, is it? There's nothing more irritating than copycat brands, and it's even more frustrating when those brands are overseas. But there's a solution. *Dum da da* cue, federal trademark registration. You can prevent the import of similar branded goods that have been manufactured overseas. Now, this doesn't stop those goods from actually being manufactured, but it does prevent them from coming into the U.S. (P.S., there's a client interview later on in this chapter that will show just how important this can be).

- *International implications, including the possibility of international registration*

If you do choose to file for trademark protection in other countries, filing in the U.S. is the first step in making that possible.

Trademark Strengths

There are five markers to describe the strength of your trademark: generic, descriptive, suggestive, fanciful, and arbitrary marks. You always want to have the strongest trademark possible, but having some protection is better than none. So let's start from the bottom.

Generic Mark

This mark is a bit of a curveball. It doesn't qualify for trademark protection unless it includes a specific detail, because it's generic. A generic trademark is a common term used to name products or services. For example, if a coffee brand is named coffee, it's a generic mark. Because of how commonly used the term is, even if it's the brand name, it cannot be trademarked. Several trademarks have lost their protection or are on the verge of losing protection due to almost becoming generic. Pampers, Velcro, Koozie, Kleenex, and ChapStick are just a few.

Descriptive Mark

A mark may qualify as a descriptive mark when it identifies one or more characteristics of a product or service and only serves to describe the product. These marks can only be registered on the supplemental registry. However, they can acquire distinctiveness to be on the principal registry. A few examples of descriptive marks are: American Airlines, DripScent, Legalpreneur, and any other term with "preneur."

Suggestive Mark

This type of mark alludes to what the word is describing but isn't that explicit. Think of brands like 7/11 or Netflix. Both suggest something about the good or service being offered, but allow the audience to use their imagination to put it together.

Arbitrary Mark

If the term or phrase you want to protect has an ordinary meaning but is being applied differently for the purpose of your business, it may be an arbitrary mark. Camel, the cigarette brand, is an example of an arbitrary mark. Camel is a familiar term. However, in this case, the word has nothing to do with the general meaning of the term. Therefore, if someone were to file Camel for breeding them, it would get refused for being generic.

Fanciful Mark

This mark is one of the easiest to obtain trademark protection for because it's typically a term made up for the purpose of the brand or product. Examples of this are Nike, Adidas, Verizon and Lexus.

I threw a lot of definitions at you there! So let's summarize. Here's a breakdown of each type of trademark, from strongest to weakest.

1. Fanciful marks (hella strong)
2. Arbitrary marks
3. Suggestive marks
4. Descriptive marks
5. Generic marks (weakest)

Make sense?

Good!

Generally, filing for trademark protection and receiving a federal registration serves three main purposes:

- Identifying your goods or services as distinct
- Legally protecting your brand from those trying to copy it
- Helps you guard against counterfeiting and fraud

Your Rights As The Trademark Holder

Although trademark protection can do a lot for your brand, it does not necessarily mean you have exclusive rights to the word, symbol or mark in general. Instead, it means you could have exclusive rights for the goods/services you're offering, so long as you have a federal trademark registration, use the mark in the appropriate way, and enforce it properly.

Consider this your step-by-step guide to trademarking your creativity:

Step One: Check yourself (before you wreck yourself). By this, I mean make sure what you are trying to trademark isn't already owned by another party. To check if it's in use or has conflicting marks, go to: https://www.uspto.gov/trademarks/ search and start your search. This step is called the clearance search, and it's only the beginning.

Your next step is to check other sources, including state trademark databases, which can be found on the Secretary of State's database and a general internet search. If another company is using the mark, check to see if it's being used in a similar industry as yours. Even if there isn't a federal trademark registration, if someone else was using the same name or something similar first, they have priority to the name. And that can cause a slew of issues for you down the road. Yes, even if you do actually get the federal trademark registration.

Step Two: *Understanding Classifications*
There are 45 classes of trademarks, broken down into 34 classes for products and 11 for services. Think of a class as a category. If a similar mark is protected under one classification, you may be able to trademark your signature under a different one. This also means that to fully benefit from trademark protection, you must register your mark under the appropriate class.

Here's a break down of the most commonly used classes for small businesses, and examples of what falls under it:

CLASS	DESCRIPTION
Class 3: Beauty Products	Includes perfumes and essential oils.
Class 5: Supplements	Includes meal replacement drinks and vitamins.
Class 25: Clothing	Includes clothing, footwear and headgear.

Classes 29, 30 & 31: Foods	Each class represents a different category of food. Class 29 = meat and processed foods. Class 30 = staple foods, including coffee and spices. Class 31 = live animals, fresh produce and grains.
Class 32: Non-Alcoholic Beverages and Beer	Includes everything from beer to bottled water and carbonated beverages. It also includes syrups used to make certain drinks.
Class 33: Wine and Hard Liquor	Alcoholic beverages including wine, liquor and hard seltzers. This class does not include beer.
Class 35: Advertising and Business	Business services, including public relations, clerical services and human resource management. Retail store services also fall under this class.
Class 41: Education and Entertainment	Includes everything from teaching and training to events showcasing sports or art, podcasting, and online courses.
Class 44: Health, Beauty and Wellness	Includes acupuncture, medical services, beauty salon services and therapy.

Remember this list is not exhaustive! Decide what classes to file under.

This part is tricky. You can register your mark under multiple classes. But there are two factors to consider: cost and use. Each class registration costs $250 under the Trademark Electronic Application System (TEAS) Plus as of when this book was written. However, for your mark to receive protection under each class, you need to be doing business in that area in interstate commerce. This means you have to be doing business in more than one state. It makes it pretty simple for online companies to qualify as being in use for federal trademark purposes. If you're a local clothing boutique, you must have locations in more than one state.

Step Three: Which Registry?

So, your mark is available. Great. Does that mean it's yours for the taking? Not necessarily. To get approved by the trademark office, it needs to qualify for registration on the United States Patent and Trademark Office's (USPTO) Principal Register or Supplemental Register.

But what is the Principal Register? Think of it as the crème de la crème of trademark protection. It's the highest level of protection. The mark must be considered inherently distinctive to qualify under the Principal Register. Meaning the mark was made for the purpose of functioning as a trademark and is otherwise meaningless. It does not need to meet that threshold necessarily. It could still qualify under the Supplemental Register - not completely useless, but not as strong as the Principal Register.

Remember the strength of the trademark discussed earlier in this chapter? For the most part, descriptive trademarks are the ones that end up on the supplemental registry.

Principal Register	Supplemental Register
• Highest level of protection. • When a mark is registered on the Principal Register, that's evidence of: validity of a federal trademark, ownership of the trademark, and a nationwide exclusive right to use the trademark in commerce in connection to how it's been registered. • If someone infringes on the owners' rights, and the owner sues, the infringer has the burden to prove that the infringing mark doesn't violate the rights of the registered owner. • Finally, a mark on the Principal Register for over five years can only be challenged under limited circumstances. It's also possible to make the mark incontestable by filing the Section 15 Declaration of Incontestability. In other words, your mark is safe from being canceled. • In summary, this is the highest level of protection.	• Does not provide the same level of protection as being on the Principal Register. • In the case of infringement, the owner would still have to prove their rights to the mark that's been infringed. • They would also need to prove to the court that they have been using the mark in relation to commerce. This is of course a costly and exhaustive process. • Registration on the Supplemental Register can be challenged at any time, for any reason, and is never incontestable.

You may wonder why anyone would even want to be on the supplemental registry if you still have to prove your case in court. For starters, some protection is better than none. When you're on the supplemental registry, most ordinary people aren't aware that there are two different registries. So if you're on the supplemental registry, most have no idea you have fewer rights. Additionally, you can still enforce your mark in many of the same ways as if you were on the principal registry.

Step Four: Prepare Your Trademark Application

Make sure you are ready to file the application before submitting your documents. You must be currently using the mark or have the intention of using the mark in the near future before applying. If you file an application with an intent-to-use and it's accepted, USPTO will issue a Notice of Allowance (NOA). Your next step is to file evidence showing that you've used the mark in commerce or in connection with the goods and services you've listed on your application. Do not forget this step! I've seen many people file an intent-to-use application and get approved all the way up to the NOA but never submit their Statement of Use.

And trust me, it's a heartbreaking nightmare. At the time of going to print, the average time for an application to be approved is a year. Imagine waiting a year to forget the very final step! If you file an "in use" application, you don't have to worry about the Statement of Use because it was filed when you initially applied.

Step Five: What To Include in Your Application

For your trademark application to be considered complete, you have to include the following details:

- Your name and address.
- The legal entity you own and your citizenship. Refer back to chapter two for a refresher on entities.
- The primary contact person's name and address who will be speaking to the USPTO regarding your application—this could be you or a trademark lawyer.
- A drawing of the mark that you're trying to register. If it's just a word or phrase that you're trying to protect, then you'll need to type in the letters of the words or phrases. If there's a design element, like a specific font or color, you'll need to draw this out to accurately depict the design and cannot rely exclusively on typed out text.
- If your mark is more than standard text, then you also need a description. It doesn't need to be long, but it should describe the significant elements of the mark.
- A list of the goods and services the mark is or will be used with. This list should correlate with the classes of goods and services available. Remember, there are 45, and you pay a filing fee for each mark in each class.
- The day you first started using this mark. It will only apply if the mark is currently in use and not if you're applying for a mark you intend to use in the future.
- A verified statement or declaration that certifies what you're claiming in the application.
- The required fee.

Congratulations! Now you're ready to file through the Trademark Electronic Application System.

Step Six: Confirmation of Filing

When your application is processed, you'll receive an email from USPTO summarizing the information you've submitted. Then, you'll receive a serial number you can use to monitor the status of your application. They will send all updates to the application via email, but you can also always look up the status on uspto.gov.

Step Seven: Responding to Office Actions

The USPTO will assign you an examining attorney who will review your file. At the time of this writing, the period for a trademark examination is eight to nine months. If the attorney finds an issue with your application, they will issue an office action. In other words, your application has been denied. They will also provide you with a reason for the decision. You will have three or six months to respond to the Office Action.

Step Eight: Publishing Your Mark

If no issue is found, your mark will be approved by the examining attorney and published in the USPTO's Official Gazette for 30 days. The Official Gazette is publicly available and will allow others to contest your mark if they believe its registration would damage their respective mark.

Step Nine: Registration *or* Submit a Statement of Use

If you filed an in-use application, you're now registered! If you filed an intent-to-use application, you would receive a Notice of Allowance. You have six months to file your Statement of Use, along with evidence showing that you've used the mark. You must also pay a filing fee when you submit this statement.

Step Ten: Use it or Lose it

Remember, if you stop using your trademark or fail to maintain your registration, your trademark could be considered abandoned. Inaction will allow others to potentially claim it. To maintain your registration, file a Declaration of Continued Use along with your Section 8 Declarations. The renewals are due every 10-11 years from the registration date, but the initial renewal is due five to six years after registration.

Trademark Infringement

By now, you know what a trademark is, how to create a strong trademark, and how to obtain a federal trademark registration from the USPTO. But one thing we haven't covered, which is incredibly important, is: what exactly is trademark infringement?

There are a crap ton of nuances with trademark infringement. I could write an entire book on infringement alone. However, since this is an overall legal book, I'm going to keep it as short and understandable as possible. This is one area where I would surely suggest consulting with an attorney if you're not sure if someone is infringing on you or if you're infringing on someone else.

Like most business owners, you may think it's any brand with the same name. Although that might be true, it's not always true. Trademark infringement occurs when there's another mark similar enough to where consumers are likely to be confused.

Let's break that down.

Infringement doesn't just occur when it's the same name. It can happen when there's anything similar. Additionally, even if it is the same name, it may not be an infringement if it's not likely that confusion would occur.

Let me illustrate.

Have you heard of Delta, the airline? What about Delta, the faucet company? Clearly, both have the same dominant portion of their name. Additionally, both companies have a federal trademark registration. And funny enough, both have similar triangular logos. How can this happen?

This is why the different classes are so important. Delta, the airline company, provides a service, and Delta, the faucet company, sells products. Because their industries and classes are so different, it's unlikely consumers would be confused that they want to purchase an airline ticket but accidentally buy a new faucet for their kitchen sink.

On the other hand, my law firm was Andrea Sager Law. Therefore, all of the names below could potentially be trademark infringement.

- The Andrea Sager Law Firm
- Andrea Sager Law Firm and Associates
- Andrew Seger Law
- Andria Seger Law Firm
- The Andrew Sager Law Firm

Catch my drift?

Similar names can be trademark infringement, and even legal names can be trademark infringement. Just because you have a legal name does not mean you're legally allowed to conduct business with that name. If you have a personal brand, you definitely need a federal trademark for your name.

As I said above, there are a ton of nuances when it comes to trademarks and infringement. Some trademarks can be straightforward, but if you're unsure, don't hesitate to reach out to a trademark attorney.

Client Profile: Elizabeth Granados, founder of House of Noa.

She attributes the acquisition of her company largely to her commitment to legally securing her brand from day one and strategically protecting her intellectual property. Here's her story.

Q. What inspired you to start your company?

I started the House of Noa in 2015. My daughter was five months old, and I had just returned to my corporate job after my maternity leave, only to find out I had been demoted.

But it was a blessing.

I cut my losses and decided it was the right time to try my hand at entrepreneurship. I couldn't spend another day working for someone else. A few months later, I launched a Kickstarter for House of Noa's signature product – a children's play mat that looked like a living room rug.

I reached my fundraising goal, but that was just the beginning. For the next five years, I worked nonstop to grow my business and sold the majority shares to a private equity group. With a new CEO in charge, I knew I was ready to start my next adventure. A year after selling my majority shares, I resigned and pivoted into the best job I could imagine – being a mother full time. I'm still a silent partner in the company, but it's been amazing to have my time back and be able to pour into my kids.

Q: How did owning your intellectual property help you sell your business?

When I started the brand, I had no idea it would turn into an 8-figure company. Honestly, I was thinking pretty small. I told myself I could maybe sell a couple of containers of rugs. I wasn't thinking that far ahead. Four months into running the business, I decided to start thinking about filing trademarks. House of Noa was originally called Little Nomad, so we filed a trademark for that name. And then we moved to copyright my patterns. It was a step-by-step process, but not without its hiccups.

The first trademark application we filed was rejected because another company had the name trademarked for the class we were filing under. Because they were a major corporation, I didn't want to poke the bear. I thought I was going to have to have a company name change. But there was a problem – in the early months of my business, I had taped an episode with *Shark Tank* where I introduced the brand as Little Nomad. What would it do to potential publicity if we were operating under a different name by the time the episode aired?

It took me almost a year to find the answer. But I realized I could register my brand as a different class. And that's what I did. I didn't need to change the name. I just filed the trademark under the class that included online stores, instead of the class for mats. I learned that sometimes with intellectual property, you need to be a little bit creative with making things work.

Q: But you eventually changed your brand name. What inspired that decision?

My business was growing, and it didn't feel like the Little Nomad anymore. I really wanted to be the house of Nomad because we had initially been Little Nomad, and I wanted to symbolize growth, but someone had already trademarked the name. And so I ended up using a variation – House of Noa, which is a Hebrew word for free-flowing movement.

Q: You also filed copyrights. What aspects of your company were copyright protected?

One of the first things I did was copyright the patterns of the mats. After the *Shark Tank* episode aired, knockoffs started popping up almost immediately. Because everything had been protected, I was able to send cease and desist letters and tell other brands they needed to stop trying to sell my product. This may not have been possible if I didn't have my IP in order.

Q: Can you tell me about one of the copycat brands?

One company tried to knock off my whole website and product line. They were a non-American company, but then they tried targeting U.S. customers on Facebook, using knock-offs of my patterns. Because they were targeting U.S. customers, I was able to send a cease and desist letter.

Q: What did you include in that letter?

I included information that showed that this other company had purchased one of my playmats, then started selling a nearly identical product. I also informed them that I was the legal copyright owner. Additionally, the other company was also trying to purchase search terms for Little Nomad, making it clear that they were aware of my brand, and trying to profit off of its likeness. After that letter, the company agreed to stop selling products in the U.S.

Q: What steps did you take in setting up your business that supported you and having your company acquired eventually?

I'm not the type of person who ever cuts corners. I like to dot my i's and cross my t's. I first met my lawyer in April 2016. I was getting ready to launch the following month. He gave me a quote on how much I would need to get started in legally establishing my business, and I budgeted for that amount in my Kickstarter campaign.

Immediately after my crowdfunding capital was released, I hired him. He helped me get set up with safety testing, packing requirements, and all of the legal documents and safety nets I needed to protect my brand. Because I had involved a lawyer from day one, every aspect of my business was properly protected and structured. I didn't take shortcuts, so there were no skeletons in the closet. When my business was ready to be acquired, I hired a separate mergers and acquisitions attorney to sell the business.

The Trademark Road Map

Here's what I love about my girl Liz. She didn't start her company knowing all the answers – she just started. Aligned action is how you build the company of your dreams. Do you want a sustainable business? Perfect, then you're going to do all the things a sustainable business needs, including taking care of legal matters by filing for a legal entity and protecting your intellectual property. Because when that multi-million dollar sale comes knocking, you want to be more than ready. Do not sleep on your trademark, folks. Even if you don't see the point right now, I promise you – more than promise you, there is one!

But let's recap:

<u>What is a trademark</u>? A trademark is generally a word, phrase, or design that identifies and distinguishes the source of the goods or services.

<u>What can be protected</u>?
- *Brand Name:* This can be the official name of your business entity or your DBA name.
- *Slogan:* This can be a phrase that the public identifies you with.
- *Logo:* The symbol you use to identify your brand.

- *Colors*: These are hard to protect, and they're usually associated with packaging.
- *Packaging*: This is known as trade dress; think of the Coca-Cola bottle.
- *Course Name*: If you have an online course, the name can be protected.
- *Podcast Name*: As long as it is a unique name, it can be protected.
- *Sounds*: Think of the ESPN sound or the McDonald's jingle.
- Blog *Name*: As long as it is a unique name, it can be protected.
- *Hashtags*: You must use this on more than just social media.
- *Legal Name*: If you have a personal brand, you need to protect your name.

So, if this is the general list of what can be protected, what can't be? Glad you asked!

- *Common Everyday Phrases*: Trademarks must be unique
- *Generic Names:* A trademark can become generic if the trademark owner does not take the necessary steps to protect the mark.
- *Phrases Used For Non-Business Purposes:* Just because someone came up with a catchy phrase doesn't mean they can protect it. They must use it for business purposes.

NOTE: Neither of these are exhaustive lists. Many things can and cannot be protected with a trademark. I just wanted you to have some examples to work with when you're thinking about your intellectual property.

BONUS: I have a comprehensive download dedicated to helping you choose a solid name for your business or new offering: *Tips for Choosing a Trademark*. Make sure to check out the resources page to get the download.

For more resources and templates, go to https://thelegalpreneur. com/legalpreneurbook-resources/

Once you decide what you want to trademark, your next step is figuring out which class it belongs to.

What Are Classes?

The trademark office issues trademarks based on different goods and services. For example, as stated earlier, we have both Delta, the airline, and Delta, the bathroom faucet brand. Therefore, you will want to file in all the classes for which you sell goods or provide services. This way, you will be protected in regard to everything you sell. Make sense?

Once that's been taken care of, your next steps are the trademark search, application and registration/maintenance. And yes, in that order! Also, take into account, it could take at least a year to be officially registered.

This process may sound daunting. But I promise, enforcing your brand is way easier and much more cost effective once you have the federal trademark registration. We will be diving into enforcement in later chapters. However, here are the top three reasons why trademark protection is one of the best things you can do for your company.

1. It protects your brand from competitors.
2. It builds trust with your client by ensuring that items with your trademark are of your brand, including social media protection.
3. Trademarks are lucrative business assets that add value to your brand.

But there are also cons:

1. If you're a new business, it could be a costly expense to trademark your brand. Between the cost of lawyers and the price of each filing under each class, it can easily cost you a few thousand dollars upfront. It depends on how many marks you have.
2. There's extensive paperwork required to trademark accordingly. It's also a lengthy process.
3. Your trademark can be disputed during your application process and after.

While there are certainly cons to be mindful of when filing for trademark protection, in most cases, the pros greatly outweigh the negatives. But there are times when trademarking is not in your best interest. This generally occurs if the mark is too generic and doesn't define or reinforce your brand identity. If you're unsure whether you should trademark, you know where to find me. That's the other thing – there's so much to learn about trademarks. Believe me, I could talk about this stuff all day. What's that saying—don't think yourself out of a good idea? That's how I feel some business owners look at trademarks. They overcomplicate things, but it doesn't have to be that way. Follow the steps above, and you should be good to go.

If you're dealing with a more complicated trademark or need additional support, you've got options! Check out the DIY trademark course from Legalpreneur, join the membership, or reach out to me via email so we can figure out what works best for you.

For more resources and templates, go to https://thelegalpreneur. com/legalpreneurbook-resources/

Chapter 6:
Copyright

"It's nice to think my ideas can still entertain and challenge people after I'm gone, but I would like the royalties for them while I'm alive." — Stewart Stafford

Copyright is another form of intellectual property law. It applies to original works of authorship fixed in a tangible medium of expression. To be subject to copyright protection:

1. You must be the author or have obtained rights from the author.
2. The work must be original and;
3. It has to be somewhat permanent.

Like with most laws, there is the general rule and then the thousand and one exceptions. This chapter focuses on the general rules. Also, it's important to keep in mind that the general rules of copyright law can actually be modified with contractual agreements. For example, although the author is the automatic copyright holder, they can contractually sign their rights to someone else.

Here's a list of works that are protected according to the United States Copyright Office:

- Architectural works
- Choreography
- Pictorial works
- Graphic designs
- Motion pictures
- Audiovisual works
- Sound recordings
- Dramatic works and any accompanying music
- Literary works
- Musical works, including any accompanying lyrics or words
- Sound recordings, including spoken word, recorded speeches and musicals

This list is surprisingly extensive. You have to know how to use it. For example, although you cannot directly protect a method or a system you've designed under copyright law, you can cover it under one of the categories listed above. For instance, a computer program cannot be registered as a system, but it can be registered as literary work.

Think of the above list as broad categories.

And here's a list of what those categories actually mean in the real world. Copyright law protects:

- Novels
- Poems

- Blog posts
- Newspaper
- Dances
- Paintings
- Drawings
- Movies
- Webinars
- Podcasts
- Photographs
- Lyrics
- Graphics
- Computer programs
- Directories
- Advertising content
- Fabric designs
- Tapestries
- Cartoons
- Drawings
- Wallpaper
- Sculptures
- Models
- Glassware
- Manuscripts

Again, this is not an exhaustive list list.

But copyright does not protect:

- Ideas, procedures, methods, systems, processes, concepts, principles, or discoveries.
- Works that are not fixed in a tangible medium (for example, an impromptu dance or spur-of-the-moment choreography).
- Titles, names, short phrases or slogans (tip: remember this could be protected as a trademark).
- Familiar symbols or designs.
- Variations of fonts, typography ornamentation, lettering or coloring.
- A mere list of ingredients or contents.

Once you register your work for copyright protection, you are given the exclusive rights to:

- Reproduce the work.
- Prepare derivative works based on the works.
- Distribute copies of the work to the public by sale or other transfer of ownership or by rental, lease or lending.
- If the protected work is literary, musical, dramatic or choreographic work, or a motion picture or other audiovisual work, you also have the exclusive right to perform the work publicly.

How is it different from trademark law? Well, for starters, copyright law protects original creative work whereas a trademark protects a brand's identity. Federal copyright protection is also generated automatically upon the creation of the work. But trademarks require registration to have federal protection. Bear in mind, there are benefits to registering your copyright as well. We'll dive into that later on in the chapter. For now, let's talk about who can claim the privileges of authorship under copyright law.

Claiming Copyright Protection

To benefit from the exclusive rights of a copyright owner, you need to have some claim on the work created. Initially, the ownership of the copyright title goes to the author who created the work. However, there are exceptions.

Joint Authors

In cases of joint authorship, the authors have an indivisible interest in the work as a whole. That means they own the entire work and share rights as the copyright holders. Work is thought to be created in joint authorship when two or more authors produce individual pieces intending to merge their contributions into one singular piece. It sounds very technical but think of it as a collaboration or co-creation. For instance, two graphic designers may create a print for a t-shirt together. If the two designers combine their talents, they are joint authors. But of course, providing the parties intended for their pieces to be joined and the two work products are indivisible.

However, suppose multiple artists create individual pieces and combine them into a final work product. As a result, they are not considered joint authors if each individual piece can be separated from the overall work. The collaborative piece can still be under a single copyright title. But it does not mean the individual artists have a share of the ownership in that title. An example of this is co-authors in a literary work. Imagine if a group of writers come together, each writing chapters for a book. In this scenario, each chapter can be considered a separate work of art.

Work Made For Hire

I know, awkward wording for a relatively simple term. Work made for hire refers to a work product created under specific terms, namely employment or another contractual agreement.

Two scenarios generally create work made for hire. Firstly, when an employee creates something as part of the employee's regular duties. Secondly, when a work product is created as a result of an expressed written agreement between the creator and a party, especially ordering or commissioning it. So let's break that down.

When is someone your employee? Basically, when you treat them like one. Do they look to you for directions and instructions? Do they follow your lead and work under you? It doesn't matter if you call them an employee – what matters is the relationship. Next, what does it mean for something to be created as part of the employee's regular duties? Essentially, it's inline with the work they were hired to do, or the daily work they do for you.

To summarize, if an employee or an independent contractor creates work under certain circumstances, even though they are the creator, for copyright purposes, the actual author is the employer or the person who commissioned the work. For example, if you hire a freelancer to write blog posts for you, the default law is that the freelancer owns the copyright to the final blog post. However, if both of you have a written contract that says it's a work made for hire, then you will own the copyright to the final product.

What Does It Mean To Be Original?

This part can get complicated, so let's keep it simple. If you created the work entirely, assume it's original. If you reworked the work product of another person, you may run into issues because the original copyright holder controls the derivative market.

Issues of originality and derivative work often come up with music – specifically, making covers and sampling. To avoid running into these complications, ensure you are correctly licensing any music or works created by another author.

How do courts determine if you are infringing on another person's work? It's called the substantially similar test, and it's exactly what it sounds like. For the copycat brand to have committed an actionable infringement, its work must include a significant amount of copyright-protected material. It's not just enough that the work is kind of similar to a protected work. It must be substantially similar.

What About The 30% Rule?

So, I often get this with my clients, and I always wonder where it came from. Who started this rumor? There's this wild myth floating around that has people convinced you can copy another person's work as long as you change 30% of it.

That's a big nope. It's way more complicated than that, but I don't want to overwhelm you with the details. Here's what you need to know. Work is considered infringement when it is substantially similar to that of another. It doesn't matter what percentage you change. If your work is more similar to another's than not, then it could be considered an infringement. But unfortunately, there's no bright line rule to say what is regarded as a substantial similarity.

To stay on the safe side, I advise not to create something based on someone else's work. Instead, be original, and you will have nothing to worry about!

The Fixation Requirements

The final requirement is that your work product is fixed. Again, don't overcomplicate this. Fixation can mean anything from recording to writing down to putting it on canvas. As long as there is a recording of your creation, it's likely subject to copyright protection.

- Reference this resource chart for potential copyrightable material in a business.

Profession	Copyrightable	Not Copyrightable
Graphic Artist	A logo or image they authentically created.	A generic term they used in a logo, without any artistic expression.
Photographer	The image itself.	The pose, the look, the outfit, basically anything that isn't the actual image captured.
Content Creator	A video created.	The short quote you said in the video.
Course Creator	The exact verbiage in an online course or on your website.	The ideas in an online course or general services listed on your website.
Writer	A passage from your book.	The general storyline of a book.
Clothing Boutique Owner	Photos you took yourself.	The overall look and feel of your website.

The Copyright Process

Now that you have more of an understanding of how copyright law works, it's time to break down how to utilize it for your business. Your work product is automatically subject to federal copyright protection as soon as it's created. As long as it's original, you are the author, it's fixed, and it fits into one of the copyrightable categories. However, if you want to be able to sue in federal court, claim statutory damages when an infringement claim arises, and recoup attorney fees and other benefits, you'll need to register your copyright federally. The following pages will walk you through that.

First, let's define registration. Think of it as the process of creating a record of your copyright with the U.S. Copyright Office. It's not a required step. However, it has significant advantages, including creating a public record of key facts, such as who the owner is and the nature of the work. Additional advantages include:

- Registration gives you the power to sue in court for infringement.
- It creates prima facie evidence that the copyright is valid – meaning, until proven otherwise, under the law, you are the legal owner of the copyright title.
- If you register your copyright and then someone infringes on your rights, you can claim statutory damages, attorney fees and costs.
- By registering your copyright, you can establish a record with the U.S. Customs and Border Protection and stop the importation of infringing copies.

The good news is that registration can be done at any time within the life of the copyright. How long does copyright protection last? A long time. Truthfully, the length of time has changed several times over the years. For now, it's currently set to the author's life, plus 78 years.

Once you register your copyright, the U.S. Copyright Office will send you a certificate that confirms your ownership and registration.

To effectively register a copyright, you must submit three things to the Copyright Office:

1. Your completed application form, either online or by paper mail.
2. The filing fee.
3. Copies of the work you are registering.

Registration #: *-APPLICATION-*
Service Request #: 1-11966615315
Mail Certificate_____
Andrea Sager

Priority: Routine   **Application Date:** November 25, 2022
Correspondent _____

      Organization Name: Legalpreneur Inc.
      Name: Andrea Sager
      Email:
      Address:

                  Registration Number
                  -APPLICATION-

Title_____
Title of Work: The Legalpreneur Podcast Everything You Need to Know About LLC's

Completion/Publication_____
      Year of Completion: 2022
      Date of 1st Publication: October 28, 2022
      Nation of 1st Publication: United States

Author_____
      • **Author:** Legalpreneur Inc.
      Author Created: Sound recording
      Work made for hire: Yes
      Citizen of: United States

Copyright Claimant_____
      Copyright Claimant: Legalpreneur Inc.

Certification_____
      Name: Andrea Sager
      Date: November 25, 2022

Page 1 of 1

Your registration becomes effective the day the copyright office receives all of the required materials for registration. There's no need to wait for the certification. But before sending the required documents, ensure that you've included all the necessary documents and fees.

The Power Of Owning Your Work

Aside from having exclusive rights to your work and its derivatives, copyright ownership is a lucrative asset for any business.

If you're a small business owner looking for a passive income stream, consider licensing some of your work. Whether it's a print, the music you've made or other digital assets and courses, owning the copyright title gives you exclusive right to your work. That means anyone using it without your permission is infringing on your work. Are you tired of people stealing your content online? Hit 'em with a copyright notice. Let them know that they can use your work and share your program for a cost. It can be challenging to protect online assets, but that's why the best business owners are the ones that are creative with their approach.

I've worked with countless clients who've come across their copyright-protected work being sold online by competitors. And often, they have the same reaction. They want the infringing party to stop selling their intellectual property. Want to know why I stop them?

The goal isn't to stop other people from stealing your intellectual property. It's to ensure that you benefit from your creativity. Therefore, instead of shutting down infringement, I encourage my clients to present a choice to infringing parties – stop infringing and pay damages or pay licensing fees.

I bet you didn't see that one coming.

Look, for many people, reposting or repurposing information they see online seems harmless. Stopping infringement altogether will be impossibly difficult. Give your brand a bigger platform, by working alongside infringers. You'll make more money, and strategically leverage brand awareness. Plus, you'll save yourself the headache and cost of chasing down infringers with cease and desists.

P.S., this is an excellent strategy for content creators who constantly have their work reposted without permission. If bigger brands want to repost your photos or videos as user-generated content, that's great visibility. But you know what's even better? Having the ability to charge them a licensing fee for their use.

Client Spotlight: James Patrick of James Patrick Photography

When I decided to write this book, there were a few clients that I knew I had to interview. James Patrick was one of them.

During the lockdown of 2020, when most creatives were struggling to make ends meet, James was making 6-figure deals. Here's how he did it.

1. **Tell us how you got here! How did you become *the* James Patrick, celebrity photographer?**

If I trace the timeline back far enough, it started in journalism. I was a journalist, and the idea was to stay a journalist, not because I loved it but because it was working for me at the time. I was a decent writer, but I didn't love reporting, so there was always his weird balance. Then I was introduced to photojournalism. It was a big pivot for me. Not only did I love creating compelling imagery, but it was also something I felt a natural draw to. I didn't know any professional photographers at the time. And because we are always inundated with images of the "starving artist," I didn't listen to myself. So straight out of college, I did what was practical and took a safe job in marketing. I spent seven years working in the field, and at the same time, I had a photo business on the side that was itching to break through the surface. Eventually, it got to a point where I was running two full-time careers. Yes, I had my marketing job, but I also had this blossoming photo career primarily within health, fitness and wellness. Then one day, I decided to take a chance on myself and my business and go all in on photography. So I quit my job and put all my energy into my photography business. This was shortly after the recession in 2008. But it took off well beyond what I could have ever imagined over the ten years.

2. Before you became a full-time entrepreneur, what did you think about attorneys?

My biggest hesitation was always that I was too small, my business didn't need an attorney, and I could not afford that kind of representation. But there were times when I remember wishing I knew more about legally protecting my business. There were a few instances as a photographer where I would see my work being used in ways I disapproved of. I also had issues where clients would back out of contracts or refuse to pay me for services rendered. It was a struggle, and extremely frustrating, especially as a freelancer, when income is already unreliable. It hurt to have my work stolen time and time again.

3. Tell me about a time when you had your photos stolen. How did you respond?

There were times when it was funny. One photo was used for a phone sex ad in a weekly newspaper. It was funny because it was never meant to be a sexy photo – it was a fashion photo! It was shot outdoors, and the woman was wearing a long skirt and sweater. It wasn't sexy at all. It was taken for a fall fashion spread in a magazine. Somehow the photo was pulled off the internet and used in a phone sex ad. But here was the problem - I didn't know whom to call because I didn't want to call the number on the ad.

Then there were also the times when it was completely accidental, and there was an opportunity there. I once had a magazine that ran one of my photos and credited another photographer by mistake. I reached out to the editor of this magazine and explained what had happened. They sent me the most sincere apology, offered a retraction in the next print and paid me what they would normally pay a photographer for a full spread. That turned into one of the best relationships with a magazine I've ever had. For the next 30 years, I shot every single one of that magazine's covers.

4. **That's where it gets tricky for me as an attorney. I have clients who have work stolen all the time. And sometimes when clients don't have much money to spend, I'll encourage them to reach out without me and explain why it's an infringement. If they ignore you, or it doesn't go well, then reach out to me. In your case, James, had you involved your attorney right away, you probably wouldn't have had that kind of relationship with them that you do today.**

Absolutely. What sets this case apart is that it was media, not advertising. When it's advertising, my usage rates are completely different because the ad is being used for monetary purposes. I've done ad campaign shoots that are high 5-figures, and I've done editorial shoots that have been hours long, but the pay is just a few hundred dollars. So It's not about the amount of time. It's about how the content is being used, how many people it's being served to and what's being sold.

In the health and wellness industry, it's usually supplementing companies that are bad for infringement. The worst case I've had to deal with was a supplement magazine that used one of my photos for the back cover of Star magazine. They must have spent north of $25,000 or more for that ad spot, and instead of shooting their own content, they took mine. Here's what happened in this instance. I shot a photo for someone, and they gave that image away to this company, and the company used it in ads. Realistically, the company probably reached out to them on IG, asking them to use the image in exchange for something like protein powder. This person clearly did not realize it was for an ad, and should have yielded them several thousand dollars at minimum. And they should have yielded me a significant pay cheque with a usage fee as well. Now, that was an egregious usage, and the company could care less. I've had this same scenario happen time and time again. The image usually isn't stolen offline but instead given away to these companies by a person I photographed. Typically, clients don't know how the photography business works or what fee structure exists. They also know that they don't own these photos. I do.

5. **I've had similar issues with clients who are boutique owners. They'll hire a photographer to shoot content for them and then come to me and ask that I send a cease and desist because the photographer is using their brand photos in their portfolio or as part of**

ads. That's when I'm like, hold up, what rights do you think you have? You don't own these photos! Then I explain that whoever takes the image owns the copyright unless they assign them to you.

That's exactly it. When you hire a photographer, you are not purchasing photos. You are buying a scope of rights to use the images. Every photographer is different. It's imperative that you understand what you have rights to before you enter into an agreement. If a client comes to me and says I want photos for a website, then the contract I'm giving them and the costs I'll charge them are specific to that use. If they say we want pictures for our website, and we want to run full-page ads in Forbes magazine, then that's an entirely different agreement, and the costs will go up. The costs go up because of the usage, not because of the time and type of photos. It's essential to have these conversations when you are hiring someone. Often, photographers will put a limit on their usage. In my company, my average usage term is three years. After three years, we'll return to our clients and ask if they want to relicense their photos. Typically, the renewal cost is lower than the initial charge unless they want to shift what they are using it for. This is how commercial photographers build residual income.

Let's say you're a digital influencer. More often than not, you are going to get one of two types of user fees from your photographer: non-commercial and non-transferable use or publicity photos. Non-commercial or non-transferable means the photos are just for you to use to promote yourself or anything you create. In contrast, publicity photos allow you to transfer these photos to someone else but for publicity use only, not advertising.

Have these conversations with the people you are hiring, so that you avoid finding yourself in an uncomfortable situation down the road. What makes this complicated is that sometimes photographers don't even know this.

6. **Exactly! I've seen that myself, and it's why it's so important for photographers and all creatives to know their legal rights. That "starving artist" narrative wouldn't exist if people took the time to understand how to become profitable as an artist.**

It opened my eyes to what a photographer could get paid in a usage fee. It isn't new work. There's no labor on the photographer's side, which helped me thrive as a business owner during the lockdown of 2020. Magazines and commercial companies were licensing my existing work. I wasn't being sent out to photograph things because I couldn't. So instead, I sent the catalog of photos I legally owned to these companies for them to choose from. And you know what I learned? That some companies will pay a 6-figure licensing fee. I could send out an email with attached photos and make 6-figures. I never thought that was possible when I started my business. This is the power of understanding your rights as a creative. Your intellectual property is an asset. Use it as such.

———

James's story is not an anomaly. It's what happens when you are legally savvy and take all the steps to protect your business and understand your rights. There is so much that you can do by owning your copyright. But please, don't just take my word for it – look at the headlines. Many world-renowned artists have publicly spoken against record labels that manipulated them out of their work. The list includes The Beatles, Taylor Swift, Poor Righteous Teachers and Kanye West. Your copyright is a significant asset in your business and should be treated as such.

For more resources and templates, go to https://thelegalpreneur. com/legalpreneurbook-resources/

Chapter 7:
Patents

"Being an independent inventor is tough. You develop a product, patent it, then you're looking for someone who will see the benefit from this technology. You assume all the investment and all the risk. It can be a challenge."

— *Lonnie Johnson*

Let me keep it real with you – patent law is not my thing. And there's a reason for that. It's a subcategory of intellectual property law, similar to trademark or copyright law, but that's also where the similarities stop. Patents apply uniquely to new inventions and traditionally protect tangible scientific inventions. As a practice, patent law is equally unique. It requires the lawyers who practice in this area to have a background in math or science and take a completely different bar exam. As a former accounting major, I never considered it because I knew my undergraduate degree wouldn't allow me to practice in this area.

So why am I writing a chapter on it? It's simple – by explaining why there are such strict requirements on who can practice patent law, you'll have a better understanding of patents, when you could need one, and the steps you need to apply for one.

The Basics

According to the USPTO, a patent for an invention is the grant of a property right given to the inventor by the USPTO. It gives you the exclusive right to make, use, and sell the invention or import it in the United States. It's crucial to pay attention to the language here. The property right given to you by the patent **does not** give you the exclusive right to make, use, offer for sale, sell or import the invention. It simply gives you the right to exclude others from doing it. To enjoy exclusive rights to your invention, you have to enforce the right given to you by the USPTO without their assistance. That's right, it becomes your job to ensure unauthorized merchants, retailers, and manufacturers aren't creating and distributing your creation without your consent. Consider this when deciding whether or not a patent is right for you. Will you have the resources to enforce your rights?

PROS	CONS
You have the opportunity to own the market and can charge higher prices as a result.	It's difficult and costly to acquire.
A lucrative business asset that could attract the right investor or buyer.	You are responsible for protecting and enforcing your patent.
You can sell licenses to your patented invention that create an additional income stream.	You hold exclusive rights only for a limited time.

Holding a patent can increase the credibility of your name as an inventor and business owner.	The technical details of your invention are publicly disclosed during the patent application process. This may mean that once your patent expires, competitors have access to recreate your creation.
Patents also encourage innovation in markets because of their exclusionary powers.	A patent is only valid for the country in the country it's issued in.

There's no short and simple answer to whether you should file a patent application for your creative endeavor. I often encourage most clients to file trademark and copyright applications, but I seldom suggest patents. Most businesses need trademarks – the same cannot be said about patents. However, if you've developed an innovative piece of technology or a never-before-seen system or process, then a patent is absolutely something you should be considering. Your decision relies on a plethora of factors, including your business objectives, market potential, access to capital, and ability to enforce your patent.

One of the most common questions I get is: *do I need a patent, a trademark or a copyright?* If you ever have this question regarding your intellectual property, flip back to this chart! I include it because I want you to have an easy reference point.

	TRADEMARK	PATENT	COPYRIGHT
PROTECTED BY	Your brand identity or product from copycat infringement.	Your invention from being made, sold, or used by others.	Your creative work from being recreated by others.
EXAMPLES OF INNOVATION	The overall look and feel of your brand. This can include your logo, color palette and packaging. The litmus test is whether it can confuse consumers.	The sale or distribution of your invention without your consent.	Song lyrics, a manuscript, a slogan etc.
BENEFITS	Exclusive rights to use the trademark.	Exclusive right to prevent others from using the patented good.	Exclusive right to reproduce, distribute, and perform the copyrighted work.

Next comes understanding your application options. There are three types of patents: utility, design and plant patents. Understand which applies to your invention before proceeding with an application. Here's a quick summary of what each type represents.

1. Utility patents apply to an invention or discovery, a new and useful process, machine, article of manufacture, composition of matter, or any new and useful movement.

2. Design patents may be granted to anyone who invents a new, original, and ornamental design for an article of manufacture; and

3. <u>Plant patents</u> may be granted to anyone who invents or discovers and asexually reproduces any distinct and new variety of plants.

Filing Your Application

Okay, so here's the thing. You can file your patent application without an attorney. Of course, if you can afford to hire an attorney, I'll always advocate for letting experts own their craft and work for you. However, under federal law, patent examiners at the USPTO are legally required to help individuals who file their applications without legal representation. So you won't necessarily have the expertise and dedication of a privately retained attorney. However, you will have someone guiding you through the process. And here's what that process looks like.

The Process

Step One: Write Down a Description of Your Invention
One of the first things I want you to do is write a step-by-step breakdown of your invention process and the prototype you are creating. Be detailed. Write out what you invented, define each attribute and diagram every angle, aspect and modification of the invention. Be as descriptive as possible. The best way to get an accurate and detailed description of your creation is by creating a prototype and documenting each process step process.

Step Two: Does Your Invention Qualify for Patent Protection? The requirements for being granted a patent are specific. USPTO does not grant patents to something that is simply an idea. Further, the idea must be original in some way and differ from existing products on the market. The USPTO will not give it patent protection if your product does not meet the originality threshold.

Step Three: Create a Business Plan

Take the time to understand how lucrative your invention could be. Remember, applying for a patent is a business decision, even if you aren't currently in business. That also means acknowledging the costs associated with obtaining a patent from the USPTO. How will you and your company recover your investment? Before beginning this process, research your market and look at your projected numbers – is it worth it?

Step Four: Carry Out a Patent Search

Similar to conducting a trademark or copyright search, here, you'll want to ensure that your invention does not already exist in some capacity. Again, similar to other intellectual property searches, you can always begin with a google search. However, in this case, you'll also want to search scientific journals, including international publications.

In your search, you will inevitably discover inventions that are similar to yours. Therefore it's important that you make a note of these inventions, and write down how yours functions differently.

Step Five: Prepare Your Application

In preparing your application, you have two options: a regular or a provisional patent application (PPA). These are drastically different options. The PPA will not give you an actual patent – it only allows you to claim a pending patent status. If you aren't ready to file a full application, the PPA is your best option. It buys you time until you are prepared to complete the requirements. All that's needed is your application fee, a detailed description of the invention and an informal drawing.

I should note that after being granted a PPA, you only have one year to file the regular patent application. If you do not file in that timeframe, you can no longer claim PPA. This is often a tactic that inventors will use to pitch their products to investors or banks.

Step Six: File the Application with USPTO

When filing your application, assure that you've included all the required information.

The Power of Licensing: How to Use Your Patent Rights

As the patent holder, you have the right to exclude others from selling, using or distributing your invention. You also have the exclusive right to allow others to sell, use or distribute in the forms of licenses. This licensing power is similar to the authority granted to trademark and copyright holders. Think of licensed Disney apparel or yoga studios.

A patent license is a contractual agreement between you, the inventor, and another party. It allows the additional party to commercially make, use and sell your patent-protected invention for a specific period. Although you can decide what rights are granted to the licensee in your agreement, typically, the deal includes payment for the license in the form of a single remittance, or royalty, for the agreed-upon terms.

There are three types of licensing agreements: exclusive licensing, co-exclusive licensing and non-exclusive licensing. Before you draft an agreement, understand the difference and the rights you give away in each contract. Here's a breakdown of the difference.

1. Exclusive Licensing: When you, the licensor, grant an exclusive license to a third party, also known as the licensee, you forfeit your right to grant additional licenses for the agreed-upon duration. This means that by granting the exclusive licenses, you subsequently forfeit your right as the inventor to sell the goods for the agreed-upon duration. However, limiting the exclusive license to a specified territory is also possible, which allows you, as the inventor, to continue selling the goods.

2. Co-Exclusive Licensing: This licensing agreement is the middle path between exclusive and non-exclusive contracts. In such an agreement, the licensor

grants a license to more than one licensee, with the understanding that there will be a limited number of licenses granted.

3. Non-Exclusive Licensing: When you want to grant licenses to multiple parties, non-exclusive license agreements are the way to go. It also allows you to continue benefiting from your intellectual property rights without limitations.

Good news – this applies to all types of intellectual property. Remember how we talked about licensing agreements with photographers in the last chapter? Yup! You can use the same strategy here.

Protecting Against Infringement

Once you've been granted a patent for your invention by the USPTO, enforcing your exclusive right is largely your responsibility. Here's how you do that.

First, remember that U.S. patents only provide protection for inventions within the U.S. border. If you want exclusive European rights, you must file a second application with the relevant European offices. Now, if someone infringes on your patent in the U.S. by selling, manufacturing or distributing your protected product, you have the right to sue the party in federal district court. You can also ask the court to order the infringer to stop the infringing act. This is called an injunction. But remember, litigation is expensive, and there are multiple steps that you need to take before you have your day in court. So it may not be worth going to court. Instead, start the process by talking to the potential infringer. Send them an email informing them that you have a patent on the product and are enforcing your rights. If communication is not successful, it's time to use a demand letter.

Patent FAQ's

1. **How do I know if my invention is patentable?**
   - Read through the getting started guides by USPTO. The patent office creates resources to help you understand the details they are looking for when determining whether an invention is worthy of patent protection. Start by learning the basics of the patent process, which we covered earlier in this chapter. Then, go to the USPTO website and search through the public disclosures database. This will give you a well-rounded idea of what sort of invention is patentable.

2. **Who can apply for a patent?**
   - Anyone who creates a piece of innovation can apply. A patent can only be applied for in the names of the actual inventors.

3. **How much does a patent cost?**

- How much you pay depends on the type of application you are filing. Generally, there are three basic fees that you are responsible for when it comes to utility patents: The filing fee, the issue fee and the maintenance fee. The filing fee is paid on application. The issue fee is remitted when you are granted the patent. And the maintenance fees are dispersed 3.5 years, 7.5 years and 11.5 years after your patent has been granted.

4. **Do patents expire?**

- Yes. Your patent rights will expire within 20 years from the date that you filed your application. However, it's possible that your patent may expire sooner, if you do not keep up with paying USPTO's required maintenance fees.

Look, I'll be honest, patents are complicated. I hardly ever advise tackling a patent application solo. If you've created something so unique that it could be eligible for patent protection, then I think you should just hire an attorney who can ensure all your legal ducks are in a row.

For more resources and templates, go to https://thelegalpreneur.com/legalpreneurbook-resources/

Chapter 8:
Compliance

"Just because you have not been caught for doing it yet, does not make what you are doing is legal."
— *Loren Weisman*

What compliance means to you and your business mainly depends on the industry that you work in. Simply put, compliance means following the rules and regulations of your respective field. It's intended to create an industry standard and ensure a baseline level of service and expectations. It affects everything from the data you collect on your website to your monthly newsletter and how you work with influencers.

Staying in compliance means you are following all the rules and regulations. Additionally, it means you are not infringing on anyone's copyright, trademarks, or patents and are fulfilling and honoring all of the contracts you are obligated to. You want to ensure that you are doing business as seamlessly as possible and following all the rules, laws, regulations and everything involved.

When I had Andrea Sager Law, there were many more rules that I had to comply with. First are the rules of professional responsibility, which are essentially the code of ethics for attorneys. There's more to it than just that, though. Each state has particular rules for attorneys to follow. Additionally, the firm was required to follow the general rules and regulations that applied to a business. They included intellectual property laws, contract ethics, data collection regulations and a few dozen others.

If you're a therapist, a licensed counselor, a doctor or part of a highly regulated profession, chances are your industry has a regulatory body that also puts out a code of ethics. Many of these industries are expanding their professional ethics to include rules on social media as well. This implies that you not only have to stay in compliance with rules to upkeep and maintain your license, but you also have to follow these rules relating to social media.

Now, if you're a clothing boutique owner, the laws you should be looking out for are state laws applying to brick-and-mortar stores, and general business rules. One tricky exception is coaches. Coaching is an unregulated industry, and many coaches come from other areas. e.g.: relationship coaches, business coaches, attorney coaches. These days, it feels like there's a coach for everything. And hey, I'm not saying they're not needed. But, because it's a largely unregulated area, you may still be required to follow the rules of your professional organization—especially the rules about marketing and social media. Err on the side of caution here. It's always better to follow more rules than less.

In my experience, small businesses usually run into a handful of compliance issues because they haven't fully transitioned into running their company as a legitimate entity. These compliance hiccups can usually be found in the following:

- Human resources
- Fraud prevention
- Cybersecurity
- Privacy breaches
- Marketing
- Infringement

This chapter may seem overwhelming at certain points, but work on it slowly. Tackle one thing at a time, and the maintenance will become simple.

Compliance And Your Website

Have you ever thought about the legality of your website? If you haven't, now is the time to start. Like, right now. This is important. And trust me, chances are, your website is not in compliance. But because you've taken the time to read this far into the book, please take the time to make sure your website is in compliance! Here's what most websites need to be in compliance with:

1. **Privacy Policy.** The aforementioned is required by law. I highly recommend placing your website's privacy policy on a page that's static, like the footer. In your privacy policy, you must disclose how your business gathers, uses, discloses and manages customer data.

2. **Terms of Use.** These terms apply to those using and visiting your website. Technically, these are not required by law. However, I highly suggest using them.

3. **Terms and Conditions.** If someone can purchase a service or product on your website, you always want to make sure that you have specific terms for the checkout. Include your refund policy, shipping, and other details about placing an order.

4. **Website Testimonials.** When using testimonials on your website, you must disclose your relationship with the endorsers, ensure that the testimonials are accurate, and get written permission from your customers. It's also important to know that you can't simply copy and paste your product or service reviews from one website onto your personal one. Typically, most websites have a clause in their Terms of Service that states that user-generated content (such as reviews or testimonials) is owned by the user and licensed to the website. Unfortunately, that means you don't have the rights to use it.

5. **Emails.** Did you know that there are rules and regulations for sending emails? When sending emails, companies are required to follow the laws and regulations outlined in both the General Data Protection Regulation (GDPR) and CAN-SPAM (U.S. law). If your company has customers in the EU, then GDPR applies to those communications. I think it's a lot easier and safer to run your business in accordance with GDPR. That way, you are following the strictest guidelines and are more likely than not following other regulations. To comply with the GDPR, you are required to keep records of recipients who opt-in to your email list, including the date they consented, what form they consented through and whether they have unsubscribed.

6. **Disclaimers.** Depending on the nature of your business, you should include a disclaimer. A disclaimer is a statement that protects your business against legal claims. It notifies users that you will not be responsible for damages arising from the use of your product, services or knowledge shared on your website.

   For example, on the Legalpreneur website, I have a disclaimer that states, *"Disclaimer: Legalpreneur is not a law firm or "lawyer referral service," and should not be a substitute for legal advice, an attorney or a law firm. Communications between you and Legalpreneur are protected by our Privacy Policy but not by the attorney-client privilege. Legalpreneur provides access to independent attorneys and legal resources to use at your discretion. However, Legalpreneur cannot offer advice, explanation, opinion, or recommendation about possible legal rights, remedies, defenses, options, selection of forms or strategies."*

7. **Photos.** This is one that people often forget. You want to verify that you are using your own photos or have a proper license from a photographer for the images you choose to use on your website and throughout your business. If you decide to use stock photos, you need to make sure that you have the correct license to use them in the manner you choose. Always pay attention to the fine print when you purchase images or download free stock images.

8. **Cookie Policy.** Nearly every time you browse a website, a screen pops up, usually within the first few seconds. This screen informs you that the page uses cookies to track you and asks if you agree. Most of us haphazardly agree without fully understanding what it means. Cookies are small files that websites use to remember things about you. It can include what you put in your shopping cart, sizing, and email login. The prompt asks you if you agree to the cookie agreement

or if you'd like to be taken to the settings to modify the data the website collects. Most people just click "yes, I accept" without reading the policy. But that shouldn't affect whether or not you have a cookie policy in place! Your policy should include a breakdown of the data you collect on your website. Here's a breakdown of what you should include:

- The user must give clear consent before any cookies are used.
- Companies must clearly show how they will use the cookie data.
- All user consent must be documented and stored.
- Website access should not be limited or altered in any way if cookie use consent is not provided.
- Users should have the ability to easily withdraw cookie use consent

9. **Copyright Notice.** It can be the copyright symbol, your business name, and the year the website was last updated. There is no longer a specific notice that must be given. If you have the copyright notice present and someone infringes, you may be eligible for willful damages. This is also how you can tell if business owners are active.

For example, the Legalpreneur website footer shows © 2023 Legalpreneur Inc.

10. **GDPR And Data Compliance.** The General Data Protection Regulation is possibly the world's strictest privacy and security law. It enforces responsibilities onto organizations anywhere, so long as they target or collect data related to people in the European Union. Essentially, you need to make sure that people can trust you to use their data fairly and responsibly. Additionally, it also requires that you comply with applicable laws and regulations.

Here's a breakdown of some of the steps you can take to ensure that you are being GDPR-compliant:

- Be aware of all the data you are collecting. It's challenging to know which rules apply to you, if you're unaware of what's coming in.
- Be transparent about the data you are collecting.
- Inform users if there is a data breach.
- Keep your privacy policy up to date.
- Regularly assess all third-party risks.
- Include a double-opt-in option for all new email list sign-ups.
- Verify the age of all users that consent to you using their data.

Legal Compliance Checklist

The tricky thing with legal is that sometimes you don't know what you don't know. Unfortunately, ignorance is not an excuse. Here's a list of aspects of your business you may need to do a health check on. For each category, look up the compliance requirements for your state to ensure you are doing the necessary work. Remember, this is a general list and may not include all the elements important to your business, nor does everything listed here necessarily apply to your company.

- If a legal entity has not been formed, review and discuss the benefits of each (LLC, corporation, etc.)
- Email marketing
- Influencer marketing
- Articles of incorporation and bylaws
- Board of directors
- Committee minutes
- Corporate structure, including affiliates and joint ventures
- Insurance coverage
- Review whether corporate registration and/or filings should be carried out in other jurisdictions
- State corporate filings
- Annual corporate report filings
- Communication with IRS
- U.S. trade controls
- Review internal and external audit procedures

- Internal control procedures
- Review representations and warranties for compliance
- Review contracts and schedule notification of contract renewal dates
- Business dealings. Are there business relationships that are not covered by a written agreement?
- If you are renting office space, check to make sure it complies with the lease
- Verify filing of all IRS and Department of Labor (DOL) forms
- Review employee manual, policies and handbook
- Equal employment opportunity and affirmative action compliance
- Employee termination practices
- Job application form and standard recruiting material
- Fringe benefits
- Review Fair Labor and Standards Act compliance issues
- Tax-qualified benefit plans
- Employment contracts and engagement agreements
- Federal requirements for documentation of citizenship of employees
- Various forms of state and federal law prohibiting various forms of discrimination
- Family and Medical Leave Act
- Review the status of trademarks, trade names, domain names and copyrights
- Sales and franchise taxes
- State tax-exempt determination letters and tax filings

- Unrelated business income
- Internet solicitations
- Federal tax law substantiation requirements

The Influencer's Introduction To Compliance

You've probably seen a few influencers in the news for violating the U.S. Securities and Exchange Commision (SEC) and Federal Trade Commission (FTC) regulations. Most recently, Kim Kardashian was fined by the SEC for failing to disclose that she was being paid to promote cryptocurrency. She was charged with "unlawfully touting" a "crypto security." She violated the rules when she promoted the crypto asset security without the necessary disclosure. She agreed to pay the $1.26 million penalty payment and help the SEC with its ongoing investigation.

So, this may surprise you, but if you earn an income from what you post on social media, there are rules you need to follow. Failure to do so can land you in serious trouble, like a whopping $1.26 million penalty.

Generally, three parties are involved in influencer marketing: the influencer, the company and the agency that brokered the agreement. So who is liable when regulations aren't followed? All of them. The compliance issue most parties run into is around ads. Specifically, what constitutes an ad and how those requirements differ in different countries.

Three major regulation concerns should be on your radar, particularly if you are an influencer:

- **Fraudulent Posts.** These are posts where you claim or allude to working with a brand when no such brand relationship exists. Some influencers have been caught doing this in the past. It's the epitome of "fake it until you make it." Influencers will lie about a campaign or sponsored post with one brand in hopes of encouraging other brands to reach out. Scammy. Stay away.
- **Fake Followers!** Who knew that buying followers could get you in legal trouble? The more followers a person has, the more authority they are typically given in their industry, which means more brand deals etc. See why it's a problem? It's fake advertising.
- **Inappropriate Content.** Issues can include smoking, alcohol and even nudity in sponsored posts relative to the age of the influencer's audience.
- **Not Disclosing The Relationship.** If you're being paid to promote a brand in your social media post, that relationship must be disclosed in the post.

Careful What You Say

When I'm thinking about working with a business, one of the first places I look is the reviews and testimonials. I mean, seriously, would you ever order from a restaurant with three stars on Uber Eats? I appreciate the good and bad reviews. But sometimes, I encounter a few that have me raising my eyebrows. Sometimes an angry customer turns into a bully. As a customer who feels as if they've been wronged, you may feel compelled to leave a bad review. No one likes feeling taken advantage of or mistreated. But there's a line between leaving a bad review and defamation. And if you cross that line, you can get yourself and your business into a lot of trouble by leaving fraudulent reviews or comments on a business's page, including a possible civil action. Defamation occurs when you damage the reputation of someone by spreading untrue information, including grossly exaggerated facts.

In 2017, a judge in Texas awarded a wedding photographer a $1.08 million defamation verdict against a couple. They were found to have posted false statements on social media about the photographer after she had shot their wedding. The photographer sued the couple in 2015 after the couple engaged in what she described as a smear campaign launched against her in an effort to destroy her business.

So what happened, and how did it end up in court? The couple didn't want to pay a $125 fee for the cover of their wedding album. The photographer wouldn't release the photos to the couple until the album cover was chosen and they paid the $125 fee. The couple was upset and decided to take their anger online and to local news outlets. Then they decided to go to the press to air their grievances. The couple made statements on social media, Yelp, blogs, and Wedding Wire and made fake profiles to post defamatory comments, including one that claimed the photographer gave the commenter AIDS. When the judgment came down in 2018, the couple was shocked. They issued the following statement:

"We are stunned. We did what consumer advocates say to do: When you are wronged, you fight back. We were unhappy with the situation, so we complained as anyone would. This court decision tells consumers not to speak up for fear of fat legal bills and painful judgments. If this is the cost of standing up for what's right, we should have given in to start with. But we hope to prevail in the end. We'd love nothing more than to put this behind us and focus on raising our five-month-old child."

There is a difference between speaking up and trying to destroy someone's business. Getting a group of friends to leave 1-star reviews or blasting people on social media is not only punishable criminally and civilly, but it is also bad juju. It could end up costing you a lot of trouble. The next time you have a bad case of Twitter fingers, ask yourself if this is worth possible legal action.

Best Practices In Ensuring Compliance

There are many rules and regulations that you need to follow, and this list continues to expand as you grow your business. So how do you keep up? Here are my tips:

1. *Schedule regular reviews*
One of the best things you can do to minimize the possibility of not being in compliance is to conduct regular reviews and

keep up-to-date with legislation. Now, that can be a full-time job. Make things easier on yourself by setting Google alerts for keywords relating to your state, your industry and relevant administrative agencies.

2. *Train your staff*
Simplify compliance regulations by making information easily accessible to your team. Documentation can look like regular online courses, in-person workshops or regular check-ins. Compliance is meant to be the standard. Treat it as such.

3. *Use technology to help you streamline and simplify the process.*
Relying on paper copies and manual data entry is much more likely to introduce errors than software to handle easily automated tasks like HR, billing, benefits and compliance paperwork.

4. *Conduct compliance audits*
As an employer, you (or your company) will be liable for the dealings of your staff. You are also responsible for making sure that they act in compliance. Offer frequent training to ensure they follow all necessary procedures and policies.

If this list is overwhelming, we can help! The Legalpreneur Membership includes compliance checklists and check-ins with your attorney so that you know you are always on top of your game. Stay ready, so you don't have to get ready.

For more resources and templates, go to https://thelegalpreneur. com/legalpreneurbook-resources/

Chapter 9:
Cease and Desists and Demand Letters

"Stop right now. Thank you very much."
— *The Spice Girls*

Cease and desist letters are something I get asked about daily. As you begin to grow and scale your business, it will be something you start thinking about more as well. Essentially, a cease and desist letter is a letter of caution, warning the recipient that they are doing something that could get them sued. The letter describes the wrongdoing and demands that the receiving party stop the conduct. It may also suggest an opportunity to negotiate, request damages, and give notice. Finally, it will inform the offending party that legal action may be taken immediately if they do not cease their conduct.

There are two different ways that a cease and desist letter can impact your business: either you're the party on the receiving end or the party sending the letter accusing the other party of wrongdoing.

When To Send A Cease And Desist

These letters are typically sent when a legal wrong is being committed by a third party, and you have the legal right to request they stop. Most commonly for online business owners, this can happen in cases of infringement of intellectual property, including copyright, trademark and patents. It can also be used to warn someone who is potentially guilty of slander, libel or contractual violations.

Here's an example I've seen time and time again: you're scrolling through Instagram and come across a post that looks familiar. It's a photo of a woman modeling a hoodie with a cute design. You don't recognize the woman, but you recognize the design because you created and filed copyright protection for it. There's no way it wasn't stolen work – the copycat brand straight up stole your design.

What are your rights here?

Well, as the legal owner, you have the exclusive right to distribute copies of the protected work to the public by sale or other means of transfer. In this case, the copycat brand printed your work on a shirt and allowed customers to buy it from their e-commerce store. This is distribution of a protected work to the public by sale. They are also transferring it digitally by reposting your design on their platform without your permission.

If another person repurposed your design and posted it, would I recommend sending a cease and desist? Likely no. In this case, simply messaging or emailing the brand and asking them to remove it may be sufficient. However, if it were a commercial brand and they were potentially making a profit off your intellectual property without the appropriate license, I would absolutely recommend sending one.

It's in your best interest to hire an attorney because cease and desist letters need to outline a legal issue or claim. A lawyer would be better able to identify the problem, and write the letter in an effectively and impactfully. However, if you can't afford an attorney, here's what you need to know.

How To Write A Cease And Desist

Every cease and desist requires the same basic information. This includes:

- Your name and address.
- The recipient's name and address.
- A clear and concise statement of what they're doing and how/why it's wrong.
- Do your best to keep emotions out of it.
- The demand, requesting the recipient stops the unlawful

behavior and whatever else you want to request.

- Request for additional information: how much money they've made from it, whom they got it from, names of other people involved, etc.
- Sent by certified mail with a return receipt requested.

Your letter must be detailed, and precisely outline what you are asking. The language needs to be actionable and direct. The recipient needs to know that you mean business. The letter should include that there will be legal consequences if the action is not stopped. It should also assert your right to the request. For example, if it's trademark infringement, show that you have legal rights to the intellectual property in question. If possible, it would also be helpful to cite case law or relevant statute, in order to emphasize what laws they are violating by engaging in their behavior.

I can't stress this part enough – do not be overly aggressive. The letter should be firm and serious but not unreasonable, asking for a million dollars. You are threatening legal action to scare them into acting, and you are simply showing that you are serious about your demand. Avoid making empty threats at all costs. Remember, your demand letter can be read in court one day. And if there is a lawsuit, the court will almost certainly require proof that you tried to settle the matter outside of court amicably. So do not make baseless accusations or try to enforce legal rights that you do not have. It won't turn out well for you.

If you're hesitant to write your own cease and desist but aren't ready to hire your own attorney just yet, the Legalpreneur community may be best for you. All of our cease and desist letters are drafted by highly-specialized attorneys who've done this work countless times. Use a legal template, and customize it to your needs to ensure you are taking action in ways that will best protect your current and future interests.

These are the type of documents we include in our contract vault, which is covered in your Legalpreneur Membership. Get yourself the proper legal documents, to protect your business with confidence.

What To Do When You Receive A Cease And Desist

In my years as an attorney, I've had many clients call me in a panic because they opened up their mailbox on a random Tuesday morning to find a cease and desist letter. I've also had clients who've received one of these letters, and ignored the warning until they were served with official court documents.

Which is the better course of action when you receive a cease and desist? Neither. Don't panic, but also, leave room for a little panic to set in. A cease and desist letter is not a court order. No court documents have been filed, and you are not getting sued, even though many receivers believe it is a lawsuit. But if you ignore the demand, you very well could end up facing a preventable lawsuit. And if you do, the judge would likely hold it against you that you ignored a letter written in good faith. Simply put, a cease and desist letter is a good faith effort to avoid the court system.

First, pay attention to what the letter says. These are the questions you should be asking yourself:

- What action are they asking you to stop?
- What legal rights are they asserting?
- Do you have any defenses?
- Are they requesting damages?
- Have they retained an attorney?

These questions should help guide how you respond. Generally, a letter will ask you to stop an action. However, the letter may also ask that you disclose any monetary gain from the allegedly illegal conduct to determine a fair settlement. In any case, here's what you should do. Take into account that I highly suggest hiring an attorney if you do receive a letter. Even if you do, the following sections will still help you.

Understand the Claim
What is the alleged grievance? Take the time to understand what right or law the claim is alleging you violated to comprehend how serious the issue is and how to proceed. If it's an issue of copyright infringement, where and how did you use the protected work? Did you sell a product you were not authorized to sell? Did you repost an image online? Did you purchase a license? Is the letter a mistake? The details matter here.

The letter also typically threatens a lawsuit or further legal action, and they may request payment from you. The aggrieved party may say, hey, you owe us this much money because of what you've done. Or, they may request more information to request a fair settlement payment. Language matters here, and so does research.

Potential Defenses

You may have a defense to the allegations in the cease and desist. That's why it's important not to panic. In cases where the letter involves intellectual property, you may have appropriately used the protected work. For instance, creating a parody out of copyright-protected work. Or, in the case of a contract breach, a legally valid reason not to honor your side of the agreement.

Here's a breakdown of potential defenses depending on the claim. We'll stick to cease and desist letters focusing on intellectual property and contract breaches.

Claim	Defense
Copyright violation	<ul><li>Fair use doctrine</li><li>Abandonment</li><li>A license</li><li>Misuse of copyright by owner</li><li>Statute of limitations</li><li>Proof that the work was independently created and not copied</li></ul>

Trademark infringement	• Parody • Fair use • Contesting registration • A license • Abandonment
Contract breach	• Statute of frauds • A contract is indefinite, with no agreed to essential terms • There was a mutual mistake in drafting the contract • Lack of capacity • Fraud • Unconscionable

To be completely transparent, I've seen numerous cases where people incorrectly rely on fair use or parody as a defense. And let me tell you, that isn't always going to work. Most of the time, people have an incorrect understanding of both defenses and get into legal trouble because of it. And even if you do qualify for these defenses, it doesn't mean you can't be sued. You still have to spend the time and money fighting the lawsuit to prove your defense.

So let's break those two defenses down.

The fair use doctrine allows someone to use another's protected work, without the owner's permission, within reason. What are the acceptable reasons? Happy you should ask! And I wish more people would. Fair use applies to teaching, critique, commentary, news reporting, scholarship or research. It's a limited list. Do you want to know what else? These are examples of what may be **considered** fair use. Just because your usage falls under one of these categories still doesn't mean it will be considered fair use in a court of law.

Now, let's break down the defense of parody. Typically in intellectual property law, parody is considered the juxtaposition of the protected image against a representation of a protected image. Under trademark law, in particular, it's a tough defense and the court will typically rely on various factors to determine whether the infringing work is actually a parody. These factors include:

- Strength of the trademarks.
- The similarity of the marks.
- The proximity of the products and their competitiveness with one another.
- Evidence that the senior user may 'bridge the gap' by developing a product for sale in the market of the alleged infringer's product.
- Evidence of actual consumer confusion.
- Evidence that the imitative mark was adopted in bad faith.
- Respective quality of the products; and sophistication of consumers in the relevant market.

When it comes to defenses, consider retaining an attorney to analyze the validity of your defense. Of course, you do not have to, and you could collect enough information on your own to respond to the sender. However, depending on the letter's seriousness and the nuances of your defense, hiring a lawyer could be in your best interest.

Pay attention to whether the letter comes from an attorney or the aggrieved party. The signature or letterhead is usually a good indicator. If the letter comes from an attorney, it may be a little more serious because the other party made a financial investment by deciding to retain legal presentation.

Preparing Your Response
If you do not hire an attorney, I suggest that you go through each point in the letter and draft an answer that is responsive to each remark. Get organized here, and take notes. What's the claim? Have you behaved in a potentially illegal way? If so, do you have a defense?

Generally, there are three potential responses: accept and comply with the request, ignore the request, or deny and defend. As discussed earlier in this chapter, I don't recommend option two.

Most cease and desist letters also include a response deadline. Although you do not have to rush a response, it's necessary to be mindful of how much time you have. At the very least, reach out to the other party to let them know you received their letter and will reach out with a substantive response soon.

When You're The Sender

What happens when you're the sender? As an attorney, when a client comes to me and says they want to send a cease and desist letter, my first step is always to gather information. Why? Because I want to make sure it's warranted. By that, I mean, is what the other party doing really a potential legal issue? No ethical lawyer would agree to send a cease and desist letter as an intimidation tactic – they should only be sent if and when there is the possibility of litigation.

I also make sure to let the client know that sending a letter does not mean the other person will stop their behavior or even respond. However, it is in the other party's best interest to act. I also emphasize to my clients that a cease and desist letter is not a court order. It has nothing to do with the courts, and frankly, if the other person does not respond, it's not illegal. All the cease and desist letter does is show an attempt to settle a conflict in good faith.

Before courts allow you to sue, they want you to make a good faith effort to settle the matter before suing. So if the other party does ignore the letter, or they are not negotiating in good faith, the court will take note of it. In that case, it's beneficial to you, because you can show the court that they are not acting in a good faith effort. Ideally, you want to be able to show all the ways you tried to find a solution outside of the courtroom.

If you do not hire an attorney, consider following the same steps I highlighted above.

Understanding Demand Letters

A cease and desist is not your only option when dealing with an unresponsive or potentially infringing party. There's also the option of a demand letter. A demand letter is a formal document, where one party demands payment or other forms of relief from the receiving party. Like a cease and desist, a demand letter is used to resolve conflict out of court. Demand letters open up a more formal discussion between you and the other party by explaining the following:

- Your grievance
- The bills or expenses that you've incurred because of their actions
- The amount or action you are requesting

Although many courts require that you try to resolve conflict out of court before filing a suit, sending a demand letter is not a legal requirement. But there are benefits to doing so. First, in many cases, a demand letter can trigger a settlement. Court is costly and exhausting. Believe me, you want to settle outside of court. If you've already tried meditating with the other party over the phone, or through other forms of communication, I encourage you to still try sending a demand letter. It's a formal and forceful way of outlining your grievance and shows you are serious about taking further action. Similar to a cease and desist, you do not need to retain an attorney to send one. However, the power of hiring an attorney is the law firm's letterhead. What's more serious than that? The good news is, with a Legalpreneur Membership, you have access to attorney-drafted documents that you can customize to suit your needs.

Here's a sneak peek at the demand letter template our members are given with their membership:

DATE
                    LAW FIRM LETTERHEAD

Via U.S. Certified Mail & E-mail
[INFO]

Dear Mr./Ms. Name:

Please be advised that I represent [COMPANY], the owner of all right, title, and interest in [WORKS NAME] ("Work"; Exhibit A) of which is covered by federal copyright protection. My client has reserved all rights in their Work, originally published on or about DATE.

It has come to the attention of my client that you have begun selling our clients Work (Exhibit B) incorporating elements that are identical to my client's Work. This constitutes copyright infringement.

My client has been and will continue to be substantially and irreparably damaged should this infringement continue. I, therefore, request that you immediately **cease and desist** from the ongoing sale and offering for sale of any and all infringing products on your website. In order to mitigate further damage to my client, the following actions on your part are **required:**

- Immediate discontinuance of the sale of infringing products;
- Immediate discontinuation of any use of our clients' Work or re-production of the Work in any form;
- An accounting of all sales made to date of the infringing products;
- An award of damages for all lost sales and profits;
- An award of attorney's fees.

Unless we receive your reply **within 5 days from the receipt of this letter,** we will presume that you do not intend to voluntarily take the necessary actions outlined above. Therefore, my client reserves the right to pursue any and all legal means necessary in order to vindicate her rights. This is a serious matter that must be rectified immediately. I remain available to discuss an amicable solution. I look forward to hearing from you soon.

Thank you for your attention to this matter.

For more information on sending demand letters, reach out to the team at theLegalpreneur.com

Now, what happens if sending the demand letter does not prompt settlement? There's still an added benefit. Sending a demand letter is an effective way of organizing your case if it goes to court.

Here are a few examples of when to send a demand letter:

- The contractor does not deliver a project on time
- Customer defaults on payments for an online program
- Client refuses to pay an outstanding invoice
- Business partner fails to honor their duties
- Vendor breaches contract terms

Tips To Keep In Mind
If you decide to write your demand letter, here are a few things to think about:

- Like a cease and desist letter, your demand letter should not be overly aggressive or forceful. Stick to the facts and legal issue at hand.
- State your damages. If there is a contract, let them know they previously agreed to these terms.
- Offer a solution. Let them know you don't want to take legal action and would rather settle this outside of court.
- Keep your writing tight. List all the facts, but don't go overboard.

- Send your demand letter via certified mail. That way, you will receive confirmation of their signing.
- Remind them of additional fees they may be responsible for if you do have to file a lawsuit.

Now, how is this different from a cease and desist? Well, in a demand letter, you aren't asking the receiving party to stop a certain action. You're asking for payment. It's that simple.

So Someone Stole Your Work. What Happens Now?

When I started my law practice in 2018, I knew my clients didn't have a large legal budget, if any at all, so I made it my goal to always help small business owners make their tiny budget go as far as possible. Here's a step-by-step guide on what to do the next time you find yourself in a copycat situation. It may not cost you any legal fees to enforce your brand.

- First, reach out to the other party. You probably don't need to get an attorney involved. Reaching out to the other party can actually save you money in the event that they honor your copyright and stop infringing after you reach out. You don't have to reach out, but it's a good idea to do so. I have found that this is often a great teaching moment for the other business owner. Just like there was a time you never had any idea about these laws, the other person may be where you once were.
- The next step is online takedowns for infringement. You can use this for both copyright and trademark.

Again, you don't need an attorney for this step. You can submit the takedowns on your own.

- Next, if they don't stop using your work, tell you to get lost, or completely ignore you, then get an attorney involved and send a cease and desist.
- Finally, your last resort is a lawsuit. Given the cost of a civil suit, this is a pricey option so let's hope it gets resolved before it gets to this step.

What To Do When A Client Doesn't Pay

There's nothing more frustrating than dealing with a client who refuses to pay what they owe. It's probably happened to you in some form or another. Maybe the client's card stopped working halfway through a year-long payment plan, or they went ghost after you sent them the invoice. Whatever the reason, you're not getting your money, and that's a problem. I have preached and preached about having rock-solid contracts, but this is when it really matters.

What happens when your client doesn't pay? Well, what does the contract say? What are your processes? In my client contracts, I always make sure that there is a contract that states that you are allowed to recoup any fees you incur to obtain payment. This includes the costs involved with hiring an attorney to send a demand letter or expenses involved in small claims court.

I always encourage my clients to reach out to their clients a few times before assuming this is an issue of non-payment. If the client goes ghost for an extended time, you can let them know that you will be sending this to your legal team if you do not hear back from them. If you still don't hear back, get your lawyer to send the letter because it works. It's something about seeing that letterhead from an attorney that gets them to sit up straight and take you more seriously.

If they don't pay even after sending the letter, consider going through a small claims court. Your decision should come down to whether it's worth it. Namely, how much are you owed? If the filing fee for small claims court is more than what you are owed, it may not be worth it for you.

I hate that I even have to say this, but, if someone doesn't pay, please don't automatically air your grievances on social media. It will rarely end well for you. It looks unprofessional and can cause more problems than it's worth. Trust me on this.
For more resources and templates, go to https://thelegalpreneur. com/legalpreneurbook-resources/

Chapter 10:
All the Way Up

"A small business is an amazing way to serve and leave an impact on the world you live in." — Nicole Snow

Picture this:

It's 2 PM on a Tuesday. You're sitting on a beach with your partner (or alone if you're as single as a Pringle like me), devouring a novel and soaking in all the sun you can. Your phone pings three times in a row, so you finally decide to check it, expecting it to be a text from your marketing team or sales lead. Instead, it's a series of emails confirming purchases that have been made in your shop. That's the beauty of properly setting up your business. It really can be as easy as it sounds. But first, you have to do the work.

In each of my businesses, I had one common goal in mind – ultimate freedom. I wanted to be at the beach on a Tuesday and take my kids to Disneyland on a Thursday without needing to request time off from my boss. It wasn't just the financial flexibility I was after. It was about owning my time again. I didn't want to ask permission to live my life on my terms because isn't it crazy that we spend our entire lives living for the weekend? It's never sat well with me. In most corporate jobs, you only really get three weeks a year that belong to you. Even thinking about it now stresses me out.

Let me be clear: we don't all want the same thing in our lives. But if you're reading this, I think it's safe to assume that you want to be your own boss and establish a wildly successful business. I can't build your business for you. I can give you the step-by-step process of how I did it, but it won't be enough. What sets your business apart is you and how you show up for yourself. It's only your dream life if it reflects the things that matter to you.

Recently, I had a conversation with another attorney friend, and I spoke with her about my goals I had for Legalpreneur and the marketing strategy I planned on implementing to get there. I then did what any good friend would do and offered her my playbook to help her grow her firm to seven figures just as quickly as I did mine.

Her response blew me away.

She said, "Andrea, I love how ambitious you are, but those aren't the goals I have for my firm."

Honestly, I was shocked. Not at her response, but how I felt the need to respond to them.

Sometimes we get so caught up in our goals that we forget other people have a different vision for their life, and that's okay. It doesn't mean that they are any less ambitious. It's just that their ambitions are leading them to different outcomes. And that's intentional. Here was a friend with the same business, more or less, who wanted a completely different outcome. It would make sense if we didn't structure our businesses the same, take the same risks, or follow the same workflow. We wanted entirely different things. I loved how honest she was with herself and with me. So often, we write off people who haven't reached our version of success as wasting their talents. But that's not true at all. Success looks different for all of us because we want different things. Simple.

We start running into complications when we let other people's goals dictate our own. And it comes up in subtler ways than you think. Think about it. Have you ever had a friend's career success make you feel a type of way? You weren't jealous, but you felt a tinge in your stomach. Maybe you started mentally spiraling, questioning your own career trajectory. Were you working hard enough? Did you want it bad enough?

The problem is that we want success but have yet to define what that looks like. So you first need to decide what you want your business to look like and act accordingly. What are your business goals, and how do they correlate with your personal goals? Some of us like working in the office with co-workers, and some of us want to spend most days at the beach or on our couch working completely alone. So you must first decide what kind of life you want and just go for it. Have a vision in mind, and refuse to settle for anything that isn't that.

Personally, I wanted more freedom. And I structured my business goals to help me get there, starting with passive income.

What is Passive Income

People get many things wrong about passive income, including what it actually is. The IRS has stringent rules on what constitutes passive income, and it's possible your side hustle may fall outside the scope.

So, what's considered passive income by the IRS? Here's a list:

- Dividends
- Royalties
- Rental income

Pretty simple, right? Passive income is earnings that you don't have to be physically present for, in order to make a profit. But it's not affiliate marketing, ebook sales, courses and other side hustles.

Client Spotlight: Kaitlyn Carlson, founder of Theory Planning Partners

People constantly ask me for business advice. More often than not, those questions center around how business owners can grow their assets. Lately, my answer has been a little different.

The truth is that many of us are still stuck in the old way of doing business. You sell a product or a service, become an expert, and are on your way to being booked and busy. The problem with that is, you aren't necessarily creating more time for yourself. Instead, you are creating more work. And hey, business is business, and sometimes it's important to be busy. But 18 hours a day is not sustainable, whether it's your business or someone else's. That's one of the reasons I've been suggesting wealth management services to more and more friends and even clients.

Meet Kaitlyn Carlson, Legalpreneur client and founder of Theory Planning Partners, a boutique wealth creation firm dedicated to helping entrepreneurs grow their wealth.

1. What inspired you to start your business?

After spending half a decade in wealth management, I recognized that the wealth management industry was failing the small business owner. It came down to the way that financial advisors were compensated. A quick lesson: financial advisors typically get paid through assets under the management model.

Their fee is a percentage of the liquid assets that they manage for the client. For example, an advisor charges 1% to handle $1 million for a client, which means he (usually "he") gets paid $10,000 per year to service that client. When the stock market goes up and the account's value grows, the advisor's compensation also goes up. The fee is taken directly from the client's investment account, so the client doesn't experience the cost unless they proactively look at their statement. This structure is highly lucrative, forcing advisors to look for large sums of liquidity to manage. If there's one thing business owners don't have much of (until they sell, of course), it's liquidity. Most business owners have 80% or more of their net worth wrapped up in the value of their business. They do not get access to sophisticated financial advice or white-glove service until they sell. In my experience, most entrepreneurs sold when they were in their 50s or 60s, which meant that they went decades without access to good financial planning advice. Therefore, they missed phenomenal wealth-building opportunities. I felt that this was wrong and that there was something I could do about it. I wanted to educate business owners earlier in their entrepreneurial journey about building wealth in a savvy and sustainable way. So I started Theory Planning Partners.

2. Why was it important for you to launch a wealth creation firm focusing on female clients?

In my time at UBS Financial Services, I worked with over 300 clients. Not one of them was a self-made woman. This really bothered me. It's been statistically proven that when women have money, they enhance the communities around them. So my mission with Theory Planning Partners was to get more wealth into the hands of women.

Additionally, women still do not have access to the same level of sophisticated advice that men do. There are remnants of the old boys club in the private wealth world where strategies and secrets are exchanged on the golf course and deals are done in steakhouses. It's unrealistic to expect that a millennial woman would have access to these conversations unless she were formerly in the investment banking or private wealth world. Therefore a big part of my mission is to bring my network and expertise to these women who otherwise wouldn't have it.

3. What is a wealth creation firm? And how can a small business work with you?

I coined the wealth creation firm because I felt it represented how we support business owners. We want to teach you how to build wealth strategically versus expecting you to come to us with $1 million in cash before you can access our financial advice. For business owners, wealth creation comes in the form of the following:

(1) Optimizing the value of your business
(2) Building personal wealth outside the business
(3) Protecting and preserving the wealth you build

Achieving these three things comes down to having a solid financial plan. So all of our clients start with a financial plan, which in its most simplistic form, answers three questions:

(1) Where are we now?
(2) Where do we want to go?
(3) How do we get there?

Things are constantly evolving between your business, personal life, and federal legislation (i.e. taxes). We act as a long-term partner to our clients to help them develop strong habits and make informed decisions in harmony with the ever-changing landscape.

As advisors who specialize in working with entrepreneurs, we also recognize that your best opportunity for wealth creation lies in the success of your business. So we take a vested interest in the health of your business. We help you build out your financial success team (i.e. bookkeeper, tax strategist, CFO, etc.) and proactively manage communication amongst these professionals. We recognize that your time is best spent in the business, not playing middlewoman amongst all your professionals.

We take clients on a case-by-case basis, and we are very approachable. Clients can visit our website to book a consultation call at any time.

4. When should a small business reach out to a wealth creation firm?

Once you start making money beyond covering your basic living expenses, you have a real opportunity to build wealth. Reach out sooner rather than later, as you never know what type of wealth-building opportunities you could be seizing! Regarding who tends to be a great fit for Theory, we typically work with women who have hit 7+ figures in their business.

5. How is a wealth creation firm different from wealth management?

The most significant difference comes down to the compensation model. Our flat fee model allows us to engage business owners earlier in their entrepreneurial journey to teach them how to build wealth. As a wealth creation firm, we take a holistic approach to the business owner balance sheet which means we focus on:

(1) Optimizing the value of the business
(2) Building wealth outside the business
(3) Protecting and preserving the wealth that we've built

To do this effectively, we must have strong communication with a business owner's financial success team (i.e. bookkeeper, tax strategist, CFO). We go above and beyond to proactively quarterback communication and planning on behalf of the business owner.

This is unique in wealth management. Due to the assets under the management model, advisors primarily focus on items (2) and (3), but item (1) is what drives the wealth of a business owner. Additionally, because business owners have very little liquidity early in their entrepreneurial journey, financial advisors are not motivated to spend a lot of time with these clients from a compensation standpoint. As a result, they essentially go overlooked by the industry until they have a liquidity event (i.e. sell) or accumulate more significant wealth in their later years. By this point, owners may have missed decades of wealth-building opportunities.

Additionally, our flat fee model allows us to remain completely objective. We enjoy helping our clients build wealth that aligns with their values and preferences. Most entrepreneurs want to invest in other asset classes outside of the public markets such as real estate. However, as previously discussed, traditional wealth management charges assets under management fees. So advisors are biased toward keeping your money in stocks and bonds because that's how they get paid. Inherently, this creates a conflict of interest.

Finally, from a definitional standpoint, I would say wealth creation is about building wealth and wealth management is about protecting and preserving it. For all intents and purposes, we help you mature from wealth creation to wealth management.

6. What are some common financial issues that predominantly affect female entrepreneurs?

Even the most successful female entrepreneurs focus on the softer side of entrepreneurship (i.e. marketing, sales, manifesting, etc.) vs talking about the hard numbers (i.e. KPIs, EBITDA, profit margins, etc.), and this hurts them when it comes to building a best-in-class business. They tend to infantilize themselves by running the business as more of a hobby vs a legitimate business, even though many have built reputable businesses! One trend we've noticed in our work is that many women have appointed their spouses to be the CFOs of their companies when:

1) The reverse would never happen.
2) They should truly have a professional in that seat instead.

I see it more amongst Gen X and Baby Boomer generations of female entrepreneurs vs millennials and Gen Z. However, it speaks to the underlying issue: women still delegate crucial financial decisions to men even when they are the breadwinners of their families. It's pretty fascinating!

7. Why is it important for small businesses to think about wealth creation outside their actual business?

It's important because we want them to avoid getting stuck in the cash flow trap! While working at UBS, owners would come to me in their 60s looking to retire. A health scare or general fatigue typically triggered this. These owners did not prioritize creating financial independence outside of their businesses, so they were dependent on its sale to secure their retirement. Often, we would have a valuation of the company done, and I would have to tell them that what they would net from selling their business after taxes would not be enough to support their lifestyle. So they got caught in what I called the cash flow trap. They were stuck in the business because they needed the cash flow. The situation happened over and over and over again. Yet, it's very avoidable with proper planning. This is my whole mission behind Theory Planning Partners. I want to educate entrepreneurs in their 30s and 40s to help them avoid this fate in their 50s and 60s.

8. What financial tips did you wish someone shared with you when you first started in your career?

The earlier you start investing, the less you have to invest. Habits build wealth and time is your greatest asset when it comes to investing.

9. Case study

Emily
Age 30
Engaged to be married
Business owner
Business revenue is $1.3 million/yr.

Emily came on board with us this past year. She thought she was working with a financial advisor, but they turned out to be an insurance salesperson. So the first thing we did was a financial plan. We organized her assets and liabilities, discussed her goals for the future, then developed a plan to get her there.

We first evaluated if there were efficiencies we could create on her existing balance sheet, which there were. She was paying a high-interest rate on two land loans. We identified that she could take out a HELOC (home equity line of credit) with a much lower interest rate. This strategic decision allowed her to pay off the loans on the land. So she now owns the land outright and she's also saving over $2,500 per month by taking advantage of what I call interest rate arbitrage. She swapped in a higher interest rate for a lower one. Strategically managing debt can save you hundreds of thousands over a lifetime when you do it correctly.

Then we addressed her multiple permanent insurance policies for which she was paying exorbitant fees. Insurance has a time and a place, but it's one of the most expensive ways to build wealth. We had her cancel three of her policies as there was no need for them, and we had her obtain a basic term policy instead. This instantly saved her over $21,000 in premiums per year. We did have her maintain one permanent insurance policy which she had already heavily contributed to. We will repurpose that as her tax free bucket down the road.

Emily is 30 and wants to be financially independent by 45. She wants the ability to spend $20,000 per month. Which means we need to start saving about $13,000 per month to hit this goal. Emily was thrilled to finally have a number she could focus on hitting. First, we worked with her chief financial officer to discuss how the business could support this personal savings goal. Then we worked with her accountant to determine how we wanted to split the contributions between tax-free, tax-deferred, and taxable saving vehicles. Then we worked with Theory's investment team. They selected a proper asset allocation (i.e. a mix of stocks and bonds) to ensure Emily's investments grow in line with her risk tolerance and a reasonable rate of return. Emily wants to retire before 59 and a half. It's pivotal that we pay attention to helping her fill what I call buckets that she can pull from before then. Because with retirement accounts, you are penalized for accessing the money before that age. This is where the art of financial planning comes in. It's not an exact science as to how much we should be putting in each bucket. Certainly, the markets, life circumstances, and business performance may change our allocations over time, but we run projections to get a basic idea of if we are tracking in line with her goals. We do this on an annual basis to ensure we are being proactive.

Importantly, Emily has been married before and has a son. She is also the breadwinner of her family. So when it comes to protecting and preserving her wealth, we spent time making sure she had proper insurance coverage and basic estate planning documents in place. We helped Emily coordinate with an attorney to develop a prenuptial agreement. She wanted to ensure she was protecting her business and was very smart, as divorce can be highly disruptive to a venture. We also had her obtain a disability insurance policy because she is the breadwinner in her house. Did you know there is a 25% chance for some type of disability to occur throughout someone's career? So the disability policy would minimize disruption and reduce stress if Emily were to experience some kind of disability. We also had her put a will, health care proxy, durable power of attorney, and a trust in place. Emily wants to make sure her son is taken care of in the event she passes away. Hence, the trust ensures certain assets pass on accordingly. Finally, Emily wants to put her son in an optimal financial position when he's older. She doesn't want him to have student loans like she did. So we opened a 529 plan for her son and determined that $800 per month would be sufficient to cover his entire tuition by the time he is of college age.

Of course, a financial plan is not something you do one time and put on a shelf. It's dynamic, fluid, and more of a process than a deliverable. As we discussed, things are constantly changing between your business, personal life, and federal legislation (i.e. taxes). Having a knowledgeable, objective, and proactive partner at your side is invaluable to help you navigate your wealth creation journey successfully.

Final Words

There is so much more that I could say about being a business owner. But if I kept writing, this book would never get published. And isn't that the realest thing about all of our businesses? There's always more to fix, more to do, and more to add. I keep reminding myself that the goal is never perfection. It's small, consistent actions.

The goal of this book was never to cover every aspect of running a business. It was to be a guide. And I hope it's been that for you. There are always more conversations to be had, more comments to share, and more to learn. For more business tips, check out the Legalpreneur podcast, or join our community over at the Legalpreneur Membership.

In nearly every podcast episode, I ask my guests their number one business tip. Here's mine: don't give up. Seriously. From all the business courses I've taken, and all the companies I've built, the one piece of advice that I've always come back to is don't give up. Consistently take inspired action because perfect does not exist. Stop waiting for perfect conditions, ideal circumstances, or a better version of yourself to show up. Magic happens when you keep putting in the work day daily, even when you don't feel like it—actually especially on those days. Unfortunately, there's no magic fix to growing your business. You can take all the classes in the world and all the masterminds but if you don't show up for yourself, none of that matters.

The best advice that I, or anyone can give you is to show up in your business as your whole authentic self, and be ready to do the work. Be great. You've got this.

The g[LAW]ssary: a practical guide for the legal side of your biz

What is The g[LAW]ssary?
You've probably heard of all of the terms included in The g[LAW]ssary, but I'm willing to bet that you need to learn what all of the terms really mean and how they apply to your business.

The goal of The g[LAW]ssary is to empower you with the necessary legal business terms that you need to sound knowledgeable and professional when conducting your business.

How should you use it?
Use The g[LAW]ssary to learn the legal side of your business that you would otherwise spend hours upon hours researching on your own! Although normal glossaries are arranged in

alphabetical order, The g[LAW]ssary terms are grouped with similar relevant terms. For those who prefer alphabetical texts, the second half of The g[LAW]ssary is grouped alphabetically.

Table of Contents

- Miscellaneous
    - Independent Contractor
    - Employee Indemnity
    - Cease and Desist Letter
    - Demand Letter
    - Business Insurance

Business Entities: A business entity is the type of organization you choose to conduct your business.

Sole Proprietor

In General: Not an organized entity.

Liability Protection: None. Sole proprietors receive no liability protection for the debts and acts of their business. For instance, if you owe a debt for your business, then that debtor can come after your personal bank account. Similarly, if you cause a car accident, the other car owner can reach your business assets.

Tax Treatment: The sole proprietor is taxed personally for profits the business makes.

Formation: No formal paperwork is required.

Note: This is the default for all businesses unless you file formal paperwork to be organized.

Limited Liability Company (LLC)

In General: This entity is only recognized by states and is the most commonly used entity for small businesses due to the cost efficiency and liability protection.

Liability Protection: Members of an LLC are protected from personal liability for the debts and acts of the LLC and the other members.

Tax Treatment: The members are directly taxed individually on their income, taking into account their share of the profits and losses. Unless you elect to be taxed as an S corp (see below), then you are taxed the same as a sole proprietor.

Formation: To be an LLC, you must file the proper paperwork with the Secretary of State.

Note: An LLC is the best type of entity for small businesses because of the liability protection and tax treatment. Additionally, there is no board of directors to deal with.

S Corp - A Taxpayer Status

A corporation or an LLC can treat this election as a flow through entity. Meaning the business itself is not taxed. Only the owners are taxed. Not all corporations and LLCs are eligible to be an S corp because certain requirements must be met. However, most small businesses qualify for S corp status. S corp tax status is often a smart choice for small businesses once the owners pay themselves a reasonable salary. You should ask your CPA about becoming an S corp.

General Partnership

In General: A partnership is two or more people that voluntarily come together to conduct business for profit as co-owners.

Liability Protection: None. Partners are personally liable for the debts and acts of the partnership. But most importantly, all partners are responsible jointly and severally for all debts and obligations of the partnership.

Tax Treatment: Partners are directly taxed individually on the income, taking into account their share of the profits and losses.

Formation: No formal paperwork is required.

Note: General partners should consider becoming an LLC or Limited Liability Partnership.

Corporation

In General: Three major pieces make up a corporation. Shareholders own the corporation and provide the capital. The board of directors make the business decisions. Officers carry about the business decisions. The same person can be a shareholder, board of director, and officer.

Liability Protection: The shareholders, board of directors, and officers are all shielded from personal liability for the debts and acts of the corporation.

Tax Treatment: The corporation is treated as a taxable entity. A corporation is a C corp by default. The most important thing about C corps is the double tax. This means the corporation is taxed and the shareholders are taxed if the corporation pays out any dividends. A C corp can make an election to be taxed as an S corp.

Formation: You must file the proper paperwork with the Secretary of State.

Intellectual Property: Certain rights in intangible property. Intellectual property includes trademarks, patents, copyrights, and trade secrets. Once certain requirements are met to obtain the rights of trademarks, patents, copyrights, and trade secrets, owners can enforce those rights and protect their intangible property using intellectual property law.

Trademark

In General: A word, symbol, or combination intended to identify and distinguish one merchant from another.

What do trademarks protect? Trademarks protect a business's brand. Additionally, trademarks protect consumers so they don't confuse them when making purchasing decisions. Trademarks ensure consumers know the source of what they're purchasing.

How to obtain protection: If you do business and use the trademark in and outside your state, you might be eligible for federal trademark protection.

Note: It's easier to obtain trademark protection if your trademark has a distinctive meaning and it isn't descriptive of what your business does—the more unique your name, the better. For example, it would be difficult to register "The Coffee

Co." for selling coffee because the trademark merely describes the good i.e. the coffee. But on the other hand, it would be easier to register "The Unicorn Coffee Co." because unicorns have nothing to do with coffee.

Note 2: If you find someone infringing on your trademark online, you do not have to sue to get them to stop their use. Once you have the registration, you can petition the online platform to terminate use without involving the courts. In this instance, registration is very helpful for online businesses.

Patent

In General: A monopoly over a particular invitation for a limited time.

What do patents protect? It protects new processes, machines, manufactures, and composition of matter. Think inventions. Patents protect inventions.

How to obtain patent protection: File a patent application with the United States Patent and Trademark Office. A lot goes into filing a patent application, and many factors may prevent a patent application from going through.

Note: Patent protection only lasts for 20 years.

Copyright

In General: Copyright protects works of art. These include literary, musical, dramatic, pictorial, graphic, and sculptural works, motion pictures and other audiovisual works, sound recordings, and architectural works, among other things.

What do copyrights protect? It awards the creator in disseminating their ideas to the public by protecting the expression of the concept. It gives a legal device to authors to give them control in the reproduction of their works after disclosure and prevent others from reproducing their expression without their consent.

How to obtain protection: There is no formal requirement for copyright protection. Any original work fixed in a tangible means of expression is copyright protected. However, copyright registration is available and has some benefits, like statutory damages.

Trade Secrets

In General: Trade secrets are formulas, patterns, devices, or compilation of information that have economic value because they are unknown to others. What do trade secrets protect? Trade secrets protect the things that copyrights, patents, and trademarks won't cover. This includes but isn't limited to formulas, sales data, market research, marketing plans, bid price information, pricing and cost information, financial statements, computer programs, customer lists, and negative information.

How to obtain protection: No form is required to obtain trade secret protection. The key is to treat the information like a secret, i.e. limit who knows the information and take measures to secure it. The Uniform Trade Secret Act allows you to sue someone who has stolen your trade secrets.

Note: Trade secrets can be anything that is important to your company. However, it must be specific to your company. It cannot be a common industry practice.

License

A permit from an authority to own or use something, do a particular thing, or carry on a trade. Licenses come up in all kinds of instances. You can have a license to use someone's intellectual property. The important thing to know about licenses is what, if any, strings are attached. They can have restrictions, and it's advisable to understand those restrictions, so you don't violate the licensing agreement. Licenses might be exclusive. Meaning you, and only you, are the one with a license. You may want a license to be exclusive, or it may not matter.

Assignment

Stepping into someone's shoes and taking on that person's responsibilities or legal rights. Assignments come up in many different contexts. Assignment hands over legal responsibilities and rights to someone else. Some things cannot be assigned, and usually, that's due to a non-assignment clause in a contract. Regarding intellectual property, assignments are very common and sometimes are contemplated with a license.

Infringement

The use of another's intellectual property without consent or permission. If someone holds a patent, trademark, or copyright, and someone uses that patent, trademark, or copyright without permission, they could be liable for infringement. There are different ways to handle the violation. Some people ask the infringing party to stop using its intellectual property, and if they stop, that's the end of it. However, others might file an infringement lawsuit. In those instances, if the case doesn't settle, a trial will determine if infringement has occurred. Damages for infringement usually amount to the harm of the use, and in some instances, damages defined by statute.

Contracts

A legally binding document that defines the relationship between two parties. Contracts have provisions that dictate what will happen in certain situations. They often have boilerplate language, which is included in almost every contract. These include arbitration clauses and entire agreement clauses.

Non-Disclosure Agreement (NDA)

A legally binding agreement to not disclose or divulge certain confidential information publicly or privately for a time. Non-disclosure agreements, or NDAs, are a good way to keep current and past employees from disclosing information you want to keep private. It could provide a business advantage or it could hurt your business if competitors knew the information. Information that NDAs protect can include schematics for a new product, client information, sales and marketing plans, or a unique manufacturing process. It can be any information you want to protect. The NDA needs to be clear on the information you want to be protected. If you signed an NDA, review it, so you don't disclose any information you agreed not to.

Non-Compete Agreements

A legally binding agreement that prevents current and past employees from working for a competing business or starting a competing business. Non-competes are a great way to keep employees from jumping ship to a competitor and sharing insight about your business with competitors. It's important to note that non-competes must be reasonable in scope and length. If you only do business in Texas, having a scope that prevents them from working anywhere in the country would not be reasonable. Also, the length of time needs to be practical. Normally two to three years is feasible. Each state has its own rules about non-competes, so it's essential to understand the laws in your state.

Service Agreement

A service agreement is an agreement between two persons or businesses where one agrees to provide a specified service to the other. Generally, a service agreement should include a description of the services to be provided, their frequency, identification of the persons or categories of persons to provide the services, the schedule or frequency of sessions of supervision or monitoring required.

Choice of Law

This provision dictates what state's law will apply if there is a lawsuit. It's imperative to ensure the state's law listed in the provision is okay with you. For instance, if you're in California, you may not want New York law to apply because you will have to get a New York attorney, fly to New York, and handle the lawsuit in New York.

Arbitration

This provision says you will agree to go to arbitration instead of a traditional court. Arbitrators are private entities designed to handle business disputes. Arbitration is cheaper and good for businesses, so most contracts with big companies include an arbitration provision. The court will uphold the arbitrator's decision as long as the arbitration provision is valid.

No Representations and Warranties

This provision provides that there were no implied or expressed promises made about the good or service. For example, if you bought a jet ski and then sued the dealer because the jet ski wouldn't go 100 miles an hour. The dealer would point to this provision saying, they never expressly promised it would go 100 miles an hour and that it's not an implied promise because jet skis don't normally go that fast.

Entire Agreement

This provision says there are no other promises and everything the parties agree to is in the contract. Ensure that everything promised will be written in the actual contract, or someone could use this provision to get out of an oral promise.

No Assignment Clause

This provision prevents the parties from assigning the rights under the contract to another party. Sometimes only one party cannot assign the contract while the other can, which is normal.

No Special Relationship

This provision says that the contract does not create any type of partnership or special relationship. It's simply a contract. Usually, this comes into play when the parties are engaging in an independent contractor relationship.

Intellectual Property Provision

Sometimes a contract grants a license to allow someone to use another's intellectual property. The intellectual property provision defines that relationship and what rights, if any, are provided to the other party.

Third-Party Beneficiaries

This provision provides that no one outside other than the parties to the contract is intended to benefit from the contract.

Waiver of Jury Trial

This is usually coupled with an arbitration agreement. The provision provides that if there is a lawsuit, you waive the right to have a jury and instead agree to have an arbitrator or judge overseeing the case.

Severability

If a court finds one provision of the agreement invalid, the other provisions will remain valid. So, for example, if the arbitration provision is struck down that won't nullify the entire contract.

Independent Contractor (IC)

A self-employed person or entity who provides services as a non-employee. When someone is an independent contractor (IC), the client does not have to follow state and federal labor laws. However, someone does not become an independent contractor simply by being labeled an independent contractor. Control is the biggest factor in determining whether someone is an employee or an IC. If the employee mandates that the party go to the employer's place of business, the employer sets an hourly pay and set work hours. Then the contractor is most likely an employee, not a contractor. This is a crucial distinction because it controls liability. An employer is liable for the acts of its employee. But a business is not liable for the acts of an independent contractor.

Employee

An individual employed for wage or salary. When a person is an employee, the employer must comply with state and federal employment laws such as minimum wage. Employment can either be at-will or contracted. Employment at-will means the employee or the employer can terminate the relationship whenever and for whatever reason. Employment can be set by contract, meaning work will be for a defined time. If either party wants to terminate the contract earlier, they must have good cause. If you do not classify someone as an employee when they should be an employee, you could be liable for many fines and back pay, including taxes. Make sure you're making the correct classification and hiring the right way!

Indemnity

Requires for one party to pay for the actions of another. For example, if A buys a widget from B for $5 and resells it to C, and the widget malfunctions and blows up in their face, then C sues A because B sold it to them and lastly, A is forced to pay $1 million. The indemnity clause makes A whole by allowing A to collect $1mm from B as the widget manufacturer. B will have to reimburse or indemnify A for the cost A had to pay to C. B may also have to pay A's court costs and legal fees along the way while A is battling in court with C.

Cease and Desist Letter

A letter requesting someone stop doing a particular action. A person normally sends a cease and desist letter when they have intellectual property. They believe someone is infringing on their intellectual property rights. Cease and desists are sometimes sent as a precursor to a lawsuit or in lieu of a lawsuit. They usually ask the person to stop the infringing use and threaten a lawsuit if the person fails to stop.

Demand Letter

A request that a party perform or refrain from performing. A demand letter can ask someone to pay or follow through with a contract. On the other hand, a demand letter can ask that someone not do something. Demand letters are normally set as a precursor to a lawsuit. If the demand is not met, then a lawsuit will follow.

Business Insurance

Just like you need health insurance for your health, you need business insurance for your business's health. Business insurance protects your establishment if your business is sued or faces property damage. Lawsuits and property can be very costly and can sink your business. Having some financial support is invaluable if your business is sued or faces property damage.

GENERAL BUSINESS TERMS

Acceleration Clause: A term in a loan agreement that requires the borrower to pay back the lender the entirety of the loan immediately. This clause is triggered by conditions outlined in the contract binding the parties.

Accord and Satisfaction: An agreement between two contracting parties to discharge a pre-existing obligation and agree to new terms. Essentially, the parties come to a compromise agreement on their own.

Alternative Dispute Resolution: Refers to any method of resolving disputes outside of the courtroom.

Articles of Dissolution: A document that's filed to formalize the existence of an incorporated organization.

Articles of Incorporation: Documents required to establish a corporation in Canada and the U.S. Filed with the Secretary of State. It includes critical details about the business, including business name and address, corporate structure, authorized shares, the registered agent's name and addresses of its incorporators.

Agency: A relationship between one party or person (the principal) and another (the agent), where the agent acts on behalf of the principal.

Bad Faith: Dishonest dealings.

Bill of Sale: A written statement confirming a buyer's purchase of property from a seller. Similar to a receipt.

Board of Directors: A group of people selected by the shareholders of a corporation who make decisions for the company.

Capital: The basic assets of your business, including cash and property, that can produce revenue.

Cash Flow Statement: A company's financial statement that measures the amount of cash entering and exiting the business through a specific period.

Certificate of Authority: A certificate granted by a state authority that allows a foreign corporation to conduct business in the state. For example, if you formed your corporation in Michigan, you would need to file a certificate of authority to do business in New York.

Contract: A legally binding agreement between two or more parties that gives each party involved a set of rights and responsibilities. Contracts can be written, expressed or oral. However, there are certain types of agreements that must be written down. See Statute of Frauds. Examples of contracts are business partnerships, licensing agreements, non-compete agreements, non-disclosure agreements and employment contracts.

Current Assets: Assets expected to be sold or used in business operations within one year. Current assets include cash, accounts receivable, stock inventory, and other liquid assets.

Current Liabilities: Financial obligations that are due within one year.

False Advertising: Untrue or misleading information that's shared to encourage someone to make a purchase.

Force Majeure: A contract term that can allow parties in a contract to cancel the agreement because of an unforeseeable circumstance. Examples are often limited to: acts of God, terrorism, war, or similarly unpredictable and uncontrollable events.

Fraud: The deliberate misrepresentation of facts to deprive someone of a valuable possession.

Fixed Costs: Business costs, such as rent, that are constant regardless of the quantity of goods or services provided.

Indemnity: To compensate another party for losses that occurred relating to a specific event. Based on a mutual contract between two parties where one promises to compensate the other in the event of loss.

Intangible Assets: An asset that is not physical. This can include intellectual property, such as trademarks, patents or copyrights.

Intellectual Property (IP): A product of human intellect that the law protects from unauthorized use by others.

Involuntary Dissolution: A method of dissolving a corporation. When company owners and shareholders cannot reach an agreement, involuntary dissolution is the final step that can be taken to resolve things. If all else fails, a court will force a sale of ownership from one partner to another or the sale of the business entirely.

Joint Venture: A combination of two or more parties seeking to develop a single enterprise or project for profit.

Limited Liability Company (LLC): A business structure in the U.S. that protects owners from personal responsibility for its debts or liabilities. LLCs are hybrid entities that combine the characteristics of a corporation with those of a partnership or sole proprietorship.

Natural Person: This term comes up in lawsuits. It may seem silly, but because a corporation is considered a "person," it's an important term. If you see the word *natural person*, it means the person being sued is a human being and not a corporation.

Partnership: A business or firm owned and run by two or more people.

Partnership Agreement: A document that governs the working dynamics of a partnership.

Professional Corporation: A corporation organized by one or more licensed persons to provide professional services and obtain tax advantages.

S Corporation (S corp): Corporations that are taxed on a flow-through basis. Tax liabilities from income are passed onto the corporation's shareholders to be declared individually.

Shareholders: A person who owns stock in a corporation.

Statute of Frauds: A statute that requires certain contracts to be in writing to be valid. In addition to being in writing, the contract must be signed by both parties who are bound by the agreement. These contracts include the sale of land, real estate transactions, agreements involving goods worth over $500, and contracts to last one year or more.

Sole Proprietorship: A form of business entity where one person owns all the assets and also assumes all the debts of the business.

Voluntary Dissolution: Occurs when a corporation's board of directors or the members of an LLC decide to dissolve a corporation voluntarily. Stockholders must vote in favor of the dissolution.

Winding Up: The settlement of debts and liquidated assets, which happens to dissolve a partnership or corporation.

Acknowledgements

To my team, Kayla and Cassie:
Thank you for sticking by my side through all the ups and downs in business and for always believing in the Legalpreneur mission.

To my parents:
Thank you for always believing in me and supporting my crazy dreams.

Lightning Source UK Ltd.
Milton Keynes UK
UKHW010606270123
416054UK00001B/325